Apocalypse Chow

Also by Jon Robertson:

The Sacred Bedroom:
Creating Your Personal Sanctuary for Spirituality,
Sensuality, and Solace

The Golden Thread of Oneness:
A Journey Inward to the Universal Consciousness

Also by Jon Robertson and Robin Robertson:

The Sacred Kitchen:
Higher Consciousness Cooking for Health and Wholeness

Apocalypse Chow

How to Eat Well When the Power Goes Out

Jon Robertson with *Robin Robertson*

Illustrated by Tanja Thorjussen

SIMON SPOTLIGHT ENTERTAINMENT

New York London Toronto Sydney

Dedicated to the victims of
Hurricane Katrina and other natural disasters.

Acknowledgments

Special appreciation goes to all the hardworking folks at Simon Spotlight Entertainment who had a hand in this project, especially Ryan Fischer-Harbage for his editorial guidance, Tanja Thorjussen for the wonderful illustrations, and Barry David Marcus for his inspired cover photography. Grateful appreciation also goes to Stacey Glick and Michael Bourret of Dystel & Goderich Literary Management, Laura Frisk, Bob Cwynar, Susan Lendvay, and the International Guild of Professional Butlers. A special acknowledgment, with trembling awe, also goes to the forces of nature that inspired this book.

S|S|E

SIMON SPOTLIGHT ENTERTAINMENT
An imprint of Simon & Schuster
1230 Avenue of the Americas, New York, New York 10020
Text copyright © 2005 by Jon Robertson
Illustrations copyright © 2005 by Tanja Thorjussen
Manufactured in the United States of America
First Edition 10 9 8 7 6 5 4 3 2 1
Library of Congress Cataloging-in-Publication Data
Robertson, Jon.
Apocalypse chow! : emergency eating for hurricanes,
blackouts, bachelors, and other disasters / by Jon
Robertson with Robin Robertson ; illustrated by Tanja
Thorjussen.—1st ed.
p. cm.
Includes bibliographical references.
ISBN-13: 978-1-4169-0824-1
ISBN-10: 1-4169-0824-2
1. Cookery. 2. Survival skills. I. Robertson, Robin (Robin G.)
II. Title.
TX714.R593   2005
641.5—dc22
2005010570

Contents

INTRODUCTION

Nobody needs to tell you that we have a shaky power grid. Hurricanes, floods, earthquakes, tornadoes, wildfires, ice storms, and even thunderstorms regularly knock out the power. We're also helpless victims of man-made disasters such as blackouts and rolling brownouts, which are caused by everything from incompetent power station workers to greedy investors. Add to that the increasing probability of the occurrence of solar flares, meteors, changes in the magnetic field, terrorist attacks, and the drunk who snaps off a utility pole up the street, and it's just a matter of time before we all find ourselves living as our ancestors once did—sweating (or shivering) in the dark and needing a shower, real bad.

A power outage can last hours, days, weeks, or longer as many Floridians will attest to after four hurricanes in 2004. They don't have to imagine life without electricity, gas, computers, cell phones, microwaves, or, even worse, food processors—they've lived it.

Life without electricity is bad for consumers, because we are walking electricity addicts. Interruptions to the power grid can send us into a frustrating period of withdrawal in which we are sometimes unable to communicate, travel, bathe, or eat properly. A power outage can turn even the lambs among us into vile, angry beasts after three days without air-conditioning. Veterans of hurricanes, along with boat people, backpackers, and campers, know how to achieve relative comfort with battery-powered lights and portable conveniences. But have you ever been imprisoned in your house without your refrigerator for two weeks? Your perishable food spoils in a couple of days; your frozen, in three or four. A large cooler and a few bags of ice can provide relief for a while, but then there's your stove. If it's electric, you're out of luck, unless you have a gas grill, charcoal grill, or a wood-burning stove.

During the summer of 1998, Hurricane Bonnie plunged my wife, Robin, and me, along with three hundred thousand other Virginians, into darkness for three days. We were hit again by Hurricane Isabel in September 2003, and after five days without electricity, I now know that I cannot thrive without air-conditioning and good food. I also realize that being prepared for a long-term disaster requires more than stashing a few extra gallons of water and finding your manual can opener. During Bonnie, Robin and I had prepared by merely bringing home some extra wine. However, by the third day we were at each other's throats and tired of eating peanut-butter crackers. This was absolutely unacceptable for Robin, a cookbook author and former chef. We were used to fabulous, fresh foods available to us on a whim from a number of well-stocked twenty-four-hour supermarkets. The next time, we swore, we'd be prepared. And we were, by observing the simple "do-fers," which I have now arranged into the chapters of this humble volume.

Natural disasters, of course, can bring destruction and the tragic loss of life, and *Apocalypse Chow!* can't help such victims or their devastating losses. However, the book can help those survivors who merely have to struggle without electrical power for days or weeks. It's for people whose houses are still safe to live in or those who have fled to the safety of a distant motel. During those times, when the Forces of Darkness pilfer one's existence, we discovered that we don't have to merely subsist; we can eat well for quite a long time—if we're prepared.

Most government or survivalist emergency food lists are pretty Rambo, pushing the unthinkable, such as canned meats—"buy fifty-two cans of Spam," one list reads. Without power for three days you could coax me to try canned soup. After a week I'd even consider instant mashed potatoes. But even if I were not already a vegetarian, the thought of a daily potted meat sandwich would be enough to make me *go* vegetarian. Nowhere on these "be prepared" lists does one find foods that can add a touch of gourmet elegance to brighten an otherwise miserable day collecting rainwater, standing in lines, or arguing with the insurance company. So for the next hurricane, which turned out to be Isabel in September 2003, we were prepared with an emergency larder that contained sun-dried tomatoes, canned artichoke hearts, quick-cooking whole grains, and dried shiitake mushrooms, along with the recommended peanut butter, bouillon cubes, and canned beans. We also had a small butane single-burner stove that saved our sanity. We cooked, sometimes just to eat up the soul-crushing wait.

When a true disaster strikes, such as an earthquake, tornado, hurricane, or man-made power-grid failure, preparing dinner is only one of many challenges. However, even during a power outage of a few days, the maddening loss of conveniences and the shortage of food can drive you over the edge.

After surviving four major hurricanes since we moved to the South in 1983, we discovered how to eat well during the gridless sojourn. In the days after Isabel we were the envy of the neighborhood. That's why I wrote *Apocalypse Chow!*—to help survivors everywhere cope with life without electricity and to eat well in the bargain.

Apocalypse Chow! provides sixty-eight recipes, carefully developed by Robin, that make the most of limited resources, ingredients, and cooking methods to produce variety, nutritional balance, and great taste. Not only that, but the book shows how to create a Well-Tempered Pantry—a stock of nonperishable foods that will get you through—along with menus and a neat trick that can be used by people who aren't even in an emergency situation: a cache of provender called the "Five-Day Wine Box," which can feed three to four people for five days and which all fits into an empty wine carton. The Five-Day Wine Box is even ideal for people who just don't like to cook, as well as for campers, boaters, and college students in exile from the comforts of home.

The Well-Tempered Pantry will elevate you to survival heaven with Robin's secrets for creating great flavors and textures in less than fifteen minutes, using recipes involving canned goods and other nonperishable sources. The recipes redefine traditionally bland survival food by providing creative ways to make delightful full-flavored soups, entrées, salads, and snacks. The recipes are vegetarian because—let's face it—who wouldn't prefer artichoke-shiitake-and-white-bean soup, couscous pilaf, or some garlicky chickpeas and tomatoes to a tasting menu of Spam, canned tuna, and canned bristling herring? (Of course, you can use such ingredients if you wish.) Each recipe has been designed for minimum preparation, cooking time, and cleanup in order to conserve precious fuel and drinkable water.

Various methods are described for making amazingly tasty meals over a butane burner. The clear instructions show when to use what's on hand when darkness strikes and how to determine when food is spoiled. Also discussed are Meals Ready to Eat (MREs), freeze-dried and dehydrated foods, and safety issues.

Advice on food preparation shows anyone how to get dinner on the table without a food processor or microwave oven (yes, it is possible). Use the handy sidebars, tips, and Resources Directory to keep your household well-fed, amused, and healthy as they guide you on stocking up in advance to get you through the "Dark Time." You will enjoy making these recipes, which you can prepare even when the electricity is on, as well as using the suggestions on ways to save your sanity should the power outage last beyond your wildest imaginings (say, three hours).

With *Apocalypse Chow!* anyone can be prepared for a storm, a blackout, a renegade comet, and even, quite possibly, the actual apocalypse.

Chapter 1

Power to the People

After a natural disaster, having to muddle along without electricity is no laughing matter; that is, unless you compare it to losing your life and property. But if you're lucky enough to escape with your hide, missing the conveniences of life as you know it can drive you mad. The days pass. You gaze upon your silent appliances, the unseeing eyes of your computer and TV, and wish you had something to eat besides another jar of salsa.

Once the beloved "juice" is gone, eating great meals can go a long way toward helping you feel better. It's especially true during a temporary lack of electrical power from a thunderstorm, a blizzard, or even some stupid human error that snafus the power grid. To illustrate, step back in time to September 18, 2003—the day Hurricane Isabel nailed Virginia Beach, Virginia.

We Did All the Right Things

The day before Isabel hit, the hurricane was already hammering North Carolina's Outer Banks. The bellies of the leaves showed white against the slate gray sky as we screwed plywood over our windows, a job that requires most of a day and a lot of cursing. The smell of ozone was in the air, and the Oceanfront was cast in a foreboding yellow glow.

Robin and I had done all the customary preparation for hurricanes that people who live on the coast generally follow: a good supply of wine, red and white, including a serviceable red zin for storm refugees who might enjoy it. We trekked out to the supermarket for extra water, food, and flashlight batteries—just in case this was the Big One. We had little luck at three grocery stores, but hit pay dirt at a fourth.

We raced up and down the aisles, the bearings on our shopping cart smoking as we blew off the crowds. In addition to the standard issue of water jugs and paper products, Robin tossed a number of food items into the cart that seemed more appropriate for a dinner party than a hurricane. "Remember Hurricane Bonnie?" she called out over her shoulder. During that storm, we had subsisted on peanut-butter crackers.

"Never again."

In the checkout line our cart stood out from those around us. Furtively judging other people's stashes (everyone peeks), we noticed a preponderance of prepared canned foods: SpaghettiOs, Spam, and Dinty Moore, along with white bread, chips, and Cheez Doodles.

Furrowed brows and disapproving silence turned our way as suspicious eyes castigated our cart full of marinated artichoke hearts, dried shiitakes, capellini, and couscous. Robin had a plan: We were used to eating fabulous meals morning, noon, and night, and no hurricane was going to reduce us to canned ravioli.

The morning of September 18, we huddled like squirrels in our dark boarded-up house just as the wind thrashed the tree boughs with powerful coughs, whipping debris around like confetti. Inside our gloomy haven we mounted our matching tropical-print La-Z-Boy chairs and flipped on the TV—the local stations had correspondents in Kill Devil Hills, Norfolk, Newport News, and Virginia Beach excitedly reporting on each gust of wind and drop of rain—but then, they generally do that anytime clouds pass over the Oceanfront.

Around noon the power died, and we were plunged into darkness and silence, save for the alto hooing of the wind. We used flashlights to find our large oil lamp with the cotton wick and soon had pioneer-grade light to keep us company.

We were already doing the usual hurricane routine: We had filled the bathtub with water, in case the water system failed (you can use that water to fill the toilet tank or wash dishes), and lined one end of the sunroom with a dozen one-gallon containers of drinking water. We kept the refrigerator closed as much as possible and the freezer inviolate, to make the frozen food last. We also had a one-burner butane stove standing by, which Robin used for cooking demonstrations.

U.S. Hurricane Trivia

The most intense U.S. hurricane was the 1935 storm that devastated the Florida Keys. The deadliest was the 1900 Galveston storm, which took more than eight thousand lives. The most expensive was Hurricane Katrina in 2005, at an estimated $200 billion.

With our recliners still facing the now-blank TV screen, we switched on our schoolbus-yellow solar radio (with a hand-crank minigenerator for cloudy days) and found a station where the local TV news anchor excitedly read reports from along the path of the Category 3 monster that was already on our doorstep. In an hour the singing wind changed to a high-pitched scream. Airborne junk thudded against our little house, but we weren't alarmed. Not yet.

We did the one thing that made sense. We opened a crisp Chardonnay and a box of Bremner wafers. We used demitasse spoons to dab the wafers with black olive tapenade and listened to the radio announcer freak out. We only became alarmed at the height of the storm when the phone started ringing. We had no power, but the phone worked. Go figure.

The first call was from a friend in Pennsylvania whom we hadn't spoken to in years.

As the storm raged outside, he asked, "You're *home*? You didn't *leave*? Are you *all right*?"

"What do you mean, are we 'all right'? We're waiting it out. Half the people on our block stayed."

"Well, the chief of police in Virginia Beach was on national news. He ordered anyone who remained behind to write their names on their forearms, so the firefighters can identify your bodies in the morning."

He may have said it on national television, but we never heard it on our hand-crank radio.

"That's news to us," I mumbled. "The wind is really loud and the rain horizontal, but don't worry, we have plenty of wine."

The Survivalist's Rule of Three

The average human being can last:

- Three minutes without air
- Three days without water
- Three weeks without food

We received calls from a cousin in Chicago, my brothers in Pennsylvania, and friends from California. The entire nation, it seemed, was prepared to kiss Virginia Beach good-bye. What did we know? We were sitting beside our oil lamp, munching Bremner wafers, and getting a buzz.

It wasn't long, however, before the wind started howling like a passing freight train. Our little house, only three blocks from the churning Atlantic, creaked and cracked under the strain. We hadn't had enough plywood to cover our backdoor window, so we took turns peering through the window at the eighty-foot pine trees at the rear of our property: They were bending over like in the cartoons. Bits of everything rocketed by in the gray blast of rain. And then we saw it: One of the trees dropped down, then slowly sank, crunching onto the corner of the roof of our cottage and smashing our fence. The top hung threateningly over our car in the driveway. Our wood stockade fence was in splinters. We wondered about the car, but couldn't see it without going outside.

That was the scariest moment, so far. But the true terror was yet to come.

Terror Strikes

In a couple of hours the wind died down to about forty miles per hour, and I ventured outside, where I met a few other pilgrims, wandering in wonder. The yards and streets were carpeted with pine needles, tree limbs, roof shingles, and other debris—you could barely see pavement at all. From the edge of our corner property, we could see far up two streets, where fallen trees blocked the way completely. Wires lay everywhere, like perciatelli.

Around the side of the house we saw that the fallen tree was resting precariously on the power line, the trunk hovering two feet above our car. One thick branch had impaled the driveway, an eighth of an inch from the right front fender. I nervously backed the car out from under it in case the power line snapped and the thing came clunking down.

But some of our neighbors weren't so lucky. The guy behind us barely escaped an oak tree, which had fallen through the back of his house. A foot-thick limb had punched through his roof, down through the first-floor ceiling, and pierced his washing machine like Excalibur. We were grateful to learn that no one in our immediate neighborhood was injured. One guy up the street had a heart attack—the ambulance couldn't get through to him for a time, but he survived.

By evening the air was calm. It turned out that Isabel was only a Category 2. All of a sudden you could see the stars. The air was still. Except for the colossal mess it was as though the hurricane had never come. The neighborhood was trashed, and some houses had been cleaved in two by trees. Fortunately for us, the actual damage to our property was minor—some missing shingles, a leaky chimney, twenty feet of crushed fence, and some broken outside lantern lights.

Little did we know that the ordeal of apocalyptic living had just begun.

That evening we regretted covering the windows with plywood. There was no power, and I wasn't about to unscrew them by hand. (Note to self: Buy a cordless drill.) We kept the hand-crank radio close by and moved our survival operation into the kitchen—it was time for dinner.

I folded napkins and poured drinks as Robin fired up the portable butane burner and made a comforting vegetable soup with the remains of our fresh produce. In so doing, we observed one of the first principles of *Apocalypse Chow!*: When the power goes out, eat up the fresh produce first and save the frozen stuff for later.

"Delicious," I said, feeling both guilty and grateful that we should be eating so well.

Fortified by the soup, we worked together on preparing the rest of the meal. Before long I was up to my elbows in minced garlic, and occupied with something besides the storm for the first time all day.

The city's water was still running, so we washed the dishes and retired to the living room, lantern and radio in hand, where, try as I might, not even my new Hubble-power bifocals would allow me to read. No TV. No books. Just the chatter of the spastic news anchor as Isabel tore up the coast north of us.

The morning after the hurricane was bright and sunny with a blue sky over a depressing disaster area. I rode my bike around the neighborhood, dodging limbs and power lines (authorities warned against such rubber-necking), and was shocked by the number of houses with trees through them as well as some miraculous "near misses." Our powerless world was a study in contrasts: One family sobbed as they picked valuables out of their smashed house while giggling boys in black wet suits biked their surfboards over to the beach to ride the storm surf.

Crushing boredom in the relentless Virginia humidity was only part of the ordeal that ensued: Color our otherwise silent neighborhood with a surreal chorus of earsplitting generators and hollering chain saws. You can only escape it inside your hot, cavelike house, so sitting out on the patio and struggling to get through a book became a test of nerves. The air was pungent with the smell of pine sap from all the snapped trees.

Word was that power wouldn't be restored for nine days. We stared into the abyss of being in a dark house in the heat and humidity, having nothing to do, with no hot water, no air-conditioning, no computers, no videos, and, unthinkably, no food processor. The hurricane now over, terror had finally struck.

Raking the yard took two days. Like everyone else, we dumped the debris at the curb, where the detritus towered six-feet high along both sides of every street—much of which would still be there three months later. We spent some of those hours on hold with the insurance company, on hold with tree services, or on hold with the power company.

But through all of that heartache, grinding boredom, and noise, we were going to eat well. We were the envy of our neighbors as we dined at sunset, three courses made with little fuss. When the hammer of fate knocks your life into powerless boredom, there is no reason why you, too, can't at least enjoy your meals.

Our Wimpy Power Grid

Mother Nature, and even bungling human beings, can knock out the power in a number of ways. Most of the following disasters, at one time or another, will periodically upset the power grid in some part of the nation, from California to New England, and from Florida to Texas. It's wise to know their nature.

Power Blackouts

If you think your precious Radarange is safe from natural disasters just because you don't live on the coast or in Tornado Alley, think again. Just consider our shaky power grid. The California power crisis threw the state into rolling blackouts in 2001, the blame pinned on greedy market manipulators. North America's worst blackout, the 2003 United States–Canada blackout, in which New York State lost 85 percent of its power, was caused by the Ohio equivalent of Mrs. O'Leary's cow. New Mexico governor, Bill Richardson, a former head of the Department of Energy, characterized the United States as "a superpower with a third-world electricity grid." More grid trouble lies ahead, according to experts, until we can afford a modern, efficient power grid, like they have in Europe.

Blackouts, and even rolling brownouts, don't usually last very long. But, unlike hurricanes, they come without warning. Major East Coast blackouts occurred in 1965; in 1977; in 1987 (in New England, during the Great Storm); and on several other occasions. Then we had the March 1989 Hydro-Québec outage: six million people had no way to use their waffle irons for nine hours. That may not sound so bad until you consider the cause: a geomagnetic storm from the sun (for these storms there's no use packing an umbrella). Scientists tell us that magnetic interference from the sun increases every year. I don't like to think about that.

If that wasn't scary enough, Earth's own magnetic pole is shifting. No kidding. The earthquake that caused the tragic tsunamis of December 2004 in South Asia altered Earth's axis. Sure, the change was tiny. But get this: According to scientists here and in Europe, Earth's magnetic field is collapsing. Since this alarming trend began about a hundred and fifty years ago, the field has already lost 10 to 15 percent of its strength, and it has begun to affect satellites. Scientists suggest that we're in for a total reversal of the lines of magnetic force—a shift in the poles. In this process the main field weakens, eventually goes neutral, and then returns with the opposite polarity. The compass will then point south!

But we're told that there's little need to panic, though the last time this happened, the dinosaurs said *"sayonara."* While the effects may not be obvious for two thousand years, the weakening magnetic field could allow harmful ultraviolet and other nasty space radiation to seep through, flummox communications, expand the ozone holes, confuse migratory animals, fry computers, and, of course, knock the power out. In the summer of 2004, University of Rochester geophysics professor John Tarduno said, "The fact that it's dropping so rapidly gives you pause." Pause, indeed. In 2009, the European Space Agency will launch satellites for Project Swarm to monitor this and other Earth phenomena more precisely. I say, "Why wait?"

Terrorist Attacks

Since September 11, 2001, organized terrorists have put the world on notice that no one will ever sleep easy again. These creeps haven't yet bombed a nuclear plant, power generating station, or dam, but it doesn't mean they don't have just such a plan tucked up their homespun woolen sleeves.

> ### Riding out a Chemical, Biological, or Nuclear Attack
> Whether you are at home, at work, or elsewhere, in these situations it may be best to stay where you are and avoid the uncertainties outside. To minimize exposure, Homeland Security's advice is to "seal the room" with plastic sheeting and tape.

Nuclear War

Who's to say some idiot won't one day start a relay of button pushing around the world?

"We won't need haute cuisine, then," you laugh.

But consider some facts. This isn't 1962 anymore. The entire world isn't likely to be blown up in an all-out, global nuclear war. If someone shoots one of these things off, it'll probably be a rogue state or the occasional hapless terrorist who assembles a dirty bomb from spare parts found lying around in Russia.

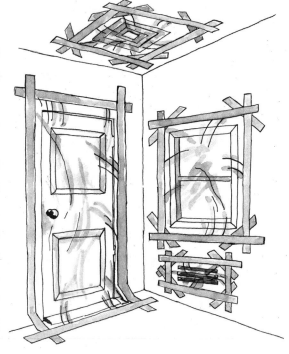

Damage and loss of life will be high at the blast site and its surroundings, of course, and radioactive fallout will plague the survivors with waves of poisoning, sickness, and cancer, depending on which way the wind blows over the next ten thousand years. Whatever the circumstances of a nuclear explosion, the power is sure to go out for quite a long time. So, in case that day comes, and you have to duck and cover, you could do worse than keep a couple of granola bars at the ready.

One more item to keep in mind, and it has happened in our neighborhood, is the event of a drunk driver, perhaps out on bail from his eighth DUI arrest, who creams a row of power poles in a 1982 Buick. Crews usually fix these within a few hours, but if it happens near the dinner hour, I believe you should still be able to eat on time.

What to Do Following a Nuclear Explosion

Should a nuclear device detonate nearby, the U.S. Nuclear Regulatory Commission advises that you move away from the immediate area, go indoors, turn on the radio, and remove your clothing and seal it in a plastic bag for later testing. Finally, take a shower to wash off dust and dirt. (Visit the U.S. Nuclear Regulatory Commission Web site at www.nrc.gov/reading-rm/doc-collections/factsheets/dirty-bombs.html.)

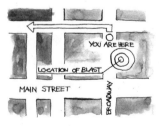

Hurricanes and Tornadoes

Hurricanes are as common on the East Coast as nuclear targets. We know the names and remember the killers: Isabel (2003), Floyd (1999), Bonnie (1998), Andrew (1992), Hugo (1989), Agnes (1972), and Camille (1969), and dozens more that have made landfall since 1900. Between two and four of these angry tempests sweep up the coast each year, often costing lives and always costing millions, if not billions, of dollars. Hurricanes invariably leave survivors without power for anywhere from a few days to a few weeks. In 2004 many Floridians endured prolonged power outages as a result of four direct hits—Charley, Frances, Ivan, and Jeanne, all within six weeks.

Tornadoes, however, are another matter, although the result is the same for survivors in that the power is lost. According to the National Weather Service Storm Prediction Center, the yearly average of tornadoes over the last three years is 1,195, and they kill an average of 49 people per year. From 2001 to 2004, twenty-three killer tornadoes have been recorded in the United States. While a hurricane wreaks equal havoc with everything in its path, tornadoes discriminate—they hop around, come and go, and can devastate the neighborhood down the street, leaving your house untouched. Twisters are a big problem in the Midwest, but you don't have to live down the lane from Auntie Em to find yourself in the path of one. Big brother and sister hurricanes spawn tornadoes as they spin, which often create some portion of the overall damage caused by hurricanes.

Tornadoes

Think quickly when a tornado is in your area. Prepare a place of refuge in advance, preferably in the basement. Otherwise, get yourself under heavy furniture in the center of the house. Stay away from windows, though you should leave them open so your 3BR 2BA ranch w/AC doesn't implode. If you are in open country, lie flat in a ditch, ravine, or culvert. Pray and, additionally, cross your fingers.

If you are lucky and still have a house, *Apocalypse Chow!* can be your best friend during the arduous period of recovery that follows a natural disaster. No doubt within days of buying this book, you will study the instructions regarding foods and supplies to stockpile and dutifully complete your shopping for the long-term items. Just before the storm season, you will buy batteries, extra water, and canned goods. So far, so good.

Power outage veterans know these can be long, agonizing, and frustrating days. You can spend hours waiting in lines for water, food, and gasoline. You will raise blisters cleaning up your yard and may even rediscover what it was like to read books. It's going to be a waiting game—waiting for insurance companies, power companies, and local officials to put everything back the way it was. After six days with no shower or TV, you will feel certain that your house must surely be next on the repair list. But not so, as you may still be a week away from being able to once again whiz basil and olive oil in your food processor. In all fairness to public officials, you can't expect to rise to the top of the list before hospitals, pizzerias, and other essential services.

During this agonizing hiatus from your life, you will either spend your time on the phone, frustrated to the point of madness, or you will gather the family and neighbors together to make an al fresco brunch, a wine tasting with canapés, or even a multicourse dinner. If the hurricane or tornado didn't blow away your tablecloths, napkins, and candleholders, you're not only going to eat well, you'll spend the aftermath enjoying the prestige of being the top back-yard chef on your street. (Best not to gloat as your hollow-eyed neighbors scoop potted meat out of cans.)

Tsunamis

The December 26, 2004, earthquake and tsunamis that devastated the Indian Ocean coastlines should stand as fair warning to anyone who lives on the coast. The United States is not immune to such catastrophes: A twelve-mile-wide piece of the Cumbre Viega volcano on the Canary Islands is loose and may fall into the Atlantic Ocean—no joke. The resulting tsunami could be seventy-five feet tall and travel across the ocean at four hundred miles per hour. If you get wind of an approaching tsunami, forget about your grill and worry about the krill. Haul butt to the mountains, pronto.

Freaks of Nature, Other

The above meteorological bugaboos take the prize as the most dangerous quirks of nature, but the power grid is interrupted regionally in various other ways. A thunderstorm can knock out power to a town or village while the burg down the road is perfectly fine. This can happen anywhere, but nor'easters (circular storms formed at sea that are unworthy of promotion to hurricanes) plague the East Coast several times a year. In the far Frozen North (above Maryland) winter storms often knock out power, though the transmission line equipment is tougher than that in the South.

Winter Storms

The next time an ice storm, or blizzard, plunges you into the dark deep freeze, you'll be prepared if you have:

- Fresh batteries in the house
- Backup for stored water and nonperishable food
- Protective clothing, mittens, and boots
- Blankets and sleeping bags
- Snow shovel and salt

In Dixie just about any freak ice storm will turn the grid into a jumble of undercooked capellini. One year while we were living in Charleston, South Carolina, such an ice storm struck. A news camera team, tracking down the salt trucks, uplinked live video of a maintenance man scratching his head.

"We got salt 'round heah somewheah," he drawled, and finally led them to a rusty old Ford F100 with eight rock-hard bags stacked on the bed. A heads-up to the unwary Yankee: In the deep South, whenever it gets icy, people drive twice as fast in order to get home quicker. . . .

Out West forest fires can wreak havoc on the power supply, and in California there's a whole lotta shakin' goin' on. Wildfires, earthquakes, and landslides can be so devastating, setting up your grill in the backyard will be the farthest thing from your mind. However, with the more manageable brush fires and temblors, you may as well dine royally while you wait for the electrons to flow.

U.S. Earthquake Trivia 2000–2003

According to the U.S. Geological Survey National Earthquake Information Center, there were only 2 quakes with a magnitude of 8.0-8.9; 27 quakes of 7.0-7.9; and 231 quakes of 6.0-6.9. Quakes registering 5.9 and below are ranked in categories from "moderate" to "very minor."

Beyond atmospheric and geological causes, outer space must be considered as a part of nature. Power losses from meteor showers, comets, and rogue asteroids are improbable, though the door is always open. What will happen then is anybody's guess. Make a mental note to avoid the direct paths of such objects.

> ## Earthquake Myth Buster
>
> During an earthquake stay away from doorways unless you live in a sturdy old house. This is because modern doorways are flimsy, and swinging doors can hurt you. Instead duck beneath a heavy piece of furniture. For further information on preparing for earthquakes, visit: http://earthquake.usgs.gov/hazards/prepare.html.

The Actual Apocalypse

Nine times out of ten when the lights go out, it isn't the actual apocalypse (the biblical prophecy of the end of the world). In the case of official Armageddon, one might question the need for preparation at all, at least regarding physical comforts. However, in the event that you gaze out your window and see what looks like the end of the world coming, it couldn't hurt to gather your extra reading glasses, a flashlight, a warm sweater, and a handheld fan. If it is the actual apocalypse, and you are one of the hapless dweebs "left behind," then you're going to be wishing for comfort food, big-time.

This list of potential disasters shows that there are more threats to our comfy lifestyles than we are prepared to face. However, even though you are likely to be visited by one or more of them during your lifetime, there is hope, glimmering like the flame beneath a chafing dish. The answer is: Be Prepared. As long as you have herbs and spices, some basic supplies, a strategy for using up your fresh and frozen foods, and some way to boil water, you have won half the battle of surviving with flair. So, we say let that power grid twitch back to life in its own good time as we open a sassy cabernet and prepare a hearty feast.

Powerless by Choice

People who choose hobbies and lifestyles in which they intentionally escape our addiction to electrical power may be the luckiest people of all when the grid fizzles out. This is because they know how to enjoy life without electricity. *Apocalypse Chow!* can inspire even the most rugged sportspeople to ratchet up the quality of their meals away from civilization.

Camping, Hiking, and Boating

It was 1976, the year of the nation's bicentennial, and Robin, our four friends, and I decided to go camping. We were townies in our midtwenties who didn't know the difference between a tent peg and a camp stove, but we bought some cheapo equipment at Kmart and went camping under the stars at Hickory Run State Park in northeastern Pennsylvania.

Along with our Tinkertoy tent (capacity: 4) and some pans, it was perfectly natural for us to bring a one-gallon Igloo cooler filled with dry Bombay martinis—one tablespoon vermouth to one gallon gin. (The noble martini was invented in the 1930s, and the 1970s marked the drink's first revival. Today the libation has risen again, like the pathetic corpse in Mary Shelley's novel, blasphemed with Kool-Aid flavors, sucked from test tubes, or slurped like oysters. Unthinkable.)

When we checked into the park, the ranger peeked through the windows of our station wagon and spotted our elegant tableware, muttering, "You folks ever go campin' before?"

"Well, *sure* we have. *Plenty* of times."

Too proud to admit that we were tinhorns, we set up camp in a Three Stooges–like manner, fumbling with struts, lines, and pegs, and starting over a couple of times. Yeah, we were amateur campers, but we were expert eaters. On our picnic table we placed two three-taper silver candelabras atop a starched white tablecloth. For dinner that first night we made linguine with a fresh tomato and basil sauce, a salad of torn greens and toasted pine nuts with a garlicky vinaigrette, and for dessert, a cherry clafouti cooked in a skillet over a wood fire. We had planned a simple dinner because we didn't know what hardships to expect. Surrounded by experienced campers who were roasting hot dogs and marshmallows on sticks, grilling burgers, or heating cans of soup, we only later began to feel self-conscious after one of us visited a neighboring campsite, asking the jackbooted occupants if they had a spare garlic press.

The above field research shows how *Apocalypse Chow!* can come in handy for a host of outdoor activities. With a little planning you can turn any rustic clearing into a Michelin four-star rated al fresco chef's table. And why not for hiking and boating? You wouldn't believe how cute and incredibly expensive the miniature pots and pans are that hikers use. Hikers can't manage to carry Granny's number twelve cast-iron frying pan and a thirty-gallon stew kettle, but these titanium beauties are light enough to help any hiker get far away from whatever they are running from before they finally collapse in a breathless heap. Hikers don't lug around canned goods, but with a basic larder of MREs (see page 68) and some dehydrated soups, you'll be able to do some passionate pan shaking out there in the bush and eat better than you ever thought possible.

Boaters have to watch their weight too, and especially their onboard stowage. That's where the techniques in this book are invaluable. The store-bought nonperishables lined up for your Five-Day Wine Box larder (see page 58) won't take up much space. Even if you are all thumbs in the kitchen, you'll dazzle your crew (salty shipmates, drunken skinny-dippers, fearless water-skiers, or weekend moochers) with recipes so easy, you'll invent delays just so those meals seem like they took longer. You'll be able to feed great dinners to the sharks in less than fifteen minutes.

Remodeling

In the winter of 2004, Robin and I were without power once again for two days. But this time it was due to another type of disaster, one of human origin. We were adding a second floor to a portion of our house (above the sunroom), installing central heating and air-conditioning, and upgrading the electrical service. The day-to-day construction was nerve-racking enough, as we'd packed ourselves into a couple of small crowded rooms for the duration. We'd been at it two months already when the day came to switch over the power. It was a task that was supposed to take three hours, but took two days instead.

We were once again determined to rely on our resourcefulness, using what we'd learned during Isabel to come through the two days well-fed and happy—at least well-fed. We whipped out some primitive writing tools (a tablet and pen), and with the help of our kerosene lamp, left over from the last hurricane, and Robin's one-burner butane cooktop, we again defeated the Dark Forces that had absconded with our precious volts and amps.

Back to School

According to Tom Wolfe's *I Am Charlotte Simmons,* painstakingly researched under the sheets of a dozen prestigious American universities, today's college students are so busy studying anatomy that they barely have time to eat. According to the sharp eyes of culinary watchdogs, when they do, these amorous youngsters are either washing down Hot Pockets with beer or spooning Cap'n Crunch at the local cereal bar.

But those kids will come up for air when they discover how easy it is to make black-bean chili, corn chowder, blueberry cobbler, and dozens of other gourmet-quality recipes in fifteen minutes on a hot plate in their dorm rooms. This also goes for students who rent a room, whose sustenance is defined by a single shelf in the downstairs refrigerator, or even the rich kids who can afford an apartment in town. While students are rarely without electricity, the sad irony is that they don't realize they can use it for cooking. The recipes in this book are so tasty and so easy to make, I fear a cult following for this book among the college crowd. But my dedication to the cause of saving young people from malnutrition forces me to promote this alternative to a diet of Cheetos and Mountain Dew. No more frying Spam in the coffee pot, pressing cheese sandwiches under an iron, or relying on that endless bowl of ramen.

We're talking quick and cheap nutrition with delicious meals and easy cleanups. So next time you hook up with someone, let *Apocalypse Chow!* be your friend with benefits—your ten-minute Orecchiette with White Beans and Olivada will be famous and provide an alibi for those sneaky one-hour tumbles between classes: "We just had dinner, that's all." You'll have your next conquest eating out of your hand.

Bachelors and Other Disasters

Certain females of the land perpetrate a myth that single men don't know how to take care of themselves properly; that their apartments are as filthy as landfills, and that their refrigerators stock little more than beer and moldy Chinese take-out cartons. So perhaps it is an added benefit of this slim edition that it will provide single men (and that rare sloppy single female who can't cook) the means for putting a balanced meal on the table in a few minutes by merely opening some cans and boxes and heating the contents. A sure sign of the apocalypse is the absentminded, stubble-chinned Knicks fan touching off a pair of long white tapers and setting before his date a meal of Instant Vichyssoise, Rosemary-Scented Bricolage, and No-Fuss Chocolate

Fondue, all made in minutes and with no appreciable knowledge of cooking whatsoever. With a little practice such an individual might even attract a permanent mate.

You'll want to use *Apocalypse Chow!*'s valuable techniques for other reasons, too. It's also handy for first-time cooks, people who don't know how to cook, studio apartment–dwellers, or those who have moved to a new place before the utilities have been connected. You will find quick and easy recipes for appetizers, soups, salads, main dishes, desserts, and snacks.

It's now time to put on some soothing music, pour a glass of wine, and explore how you, too, can flaunt your epicurean independence in the face of imposed or elected power deprivation.

Chapter 2

The Calm Before the Storm

If your power goes out because of some technical glitch, such as a blackout, odds are you won't have to evacuate. In the case of a tornado you won't have enough warning to evacuate, because twisters are unpredictable; precisely where they're going to strike is unknown until they touch down. Earthquakes are unpredictable too; other than permanently fleeing the West Coast, what's a nervous Californian to do? But with an approaching hurricane, flood, or wildfire, authorities can track the direction and generally give two types of instruction: *urge* evacuation by way of a warning, or force a mandatory evacuation. Whether you hightail it out of there or stay and take your chances, you can take specific steps to keep ahead of the game and ensure your comfort and safety.

Should I Stay or Should I Go?

When the authorities issue a mandatory evacuation, you can bet they have good reason. Their concern is your safety and health. However, humankind is made up of wise people, fools, scaredy-cats, rebels, drooling looters, and macho types who will never back down from a dare. In Chapter 1 you no doubt noted how half our neighborhood ignored the order to evacuate before Hurricane Isabel tore Virginia Beach a new jejunum. You may also recall our foolish emphasis on wine instead of safety. Clearly, we cannot be counted among the first category of humankind just noted. But at the height of the storm, we reflected. We asked ourselves what would make otherwise responsible people endanger themselves like that?

The answer isn't simple. I can speak for my own household by saying that as writers our business is in our home, where we hoard all of our important materials, manuscripts, computers, contracts, records, and our voluminous research library. For us and our generally nervous dispositions the Disaster Supply Kit described later in this chapter would have had to be the size of a semitrailer to carry all the precious ephemera that we consider vital to our livelihood.

Having moved from Charleston, South Carolina, to Virginia Beach just four months before Hurricane Hugo wiped it out, we heard many horror stories about people returning home after they had evacuated. One fortunate family returned to find their house untouched despite the fact that all the towering pines in the front yard fell down pointing north, and all the towering pines in the backyard fell down pointing south.

But others weren't so lucky. It took days for the roads to open. Bridges were out too, and by the time people returned home, materials they might have been able to save had been either ruined by subsequent bad weather or stolen by looters. Beyond Charleston Harbor lies a number of classy barrier islands that became isolated due to a downed bridge. For days after the storm had passed, authorities forbade residents to return to their homes. While the marine police patrolled one side of an island, thieves were pulling an Allied Van Lines with boats on the other side. The police couldn't stop the thieves, but neither could they allow residents to go home and defend their property.

Top Safety Tips for a Blackout

- Use only a flashlight for emergency lighting. Never use candles!
- Turn off electrical equipment in use when the power went out
- Avoid opening the refrigerator and freezer
- Don't run generators inside a home or a garage
- Leave one light on so you know when the power returns
- Listen to local radio and television

(Courtesy of the American Red Cross, www.redcross.org/services/disaster/0,1082,0_133_,00.html)

Robin and I were well aware of that problem down in the low country and in other hurricane zones, but we didn't really need such stories to make us afraid to evacuate. We're dyed-in-the-wool homebodies. Agoraphobic, even. We're also too attached to our creature comforts to readily pack up one measly carload of stuff and either flee the region or, God forbid, bunk down on cots among miscellaneous refugees spread out in the makeshift barracks of an elementary-school gym. We're not snobs, exactly, though we have observed snobbery up close. We don't think we're better than anybody either; we're just self-conscious in our jammies. We don't even like to share a bathroom with each other. We abhor noise and are phobic about germs.

Such was the minestrone of our feelings as we barricaded ourselves inside our house before that four-hundred-mile-in-diameter fiend, Isabel, blew in. However, during the worst of it we had serious doubts that we'd made the right decision. As we sneaked peeks out the one unboarded window, we noticed a guy sitting on his porch, nursing a beer, watching the trees disappear as though some giant gopher were pulling them asunder.

We aren't quite that crazy; or perhaps we're crazy in another way. However, we are absolutely certain that we would now evacuate with a Category 3 or higher. We saw enough with the Category 2 to know we wouldn't willingly risk anything worse than that. We were lucky during Isabel, because hurricanes can unpredictably gain strength or change direction in a span of hours. Such was the case with Hurricane Bonnie. We went to bed confident that she was heading out to sea, only to awaken at midnight to find ourselves in the midst of it. We advise everyone to err on the side of caution with hurricanes and, as with any other destructive phenomena, to seek a safe shelter or leave town whenever you are warned to do so.

Whether you entrench in your home or get the heck out of Dodge, there are things you can do to prepare—preparations that you will be glad you made.

Good-bye, House

When officials order you to evacuate, you'd better do what they say, or at the last minute you may find your gallantry has fled and you're drawing a blank on what you should take with you. If the storm is bad, you will wish you had taken every item that's vital to your well-being—at least as much of it as will fit in your car. If you wait until the storm arrives, it'll be too late, because this type of planning takes time and thought.

So, well before another major loss of power hits your area, do what we recently did at our house: assemble a Disaster Supply Kit, like the National Weather Service tells you to do. This box is a centralized cache of your most important papers and other things that you may need to quickly access, whether you stay home or flee from danger. Ours is a twenty-gallon plastic tub with a snug snap-on lid that can be quickly loaded into the trunk of the car. It contains the documents and other items that will ensure our fiscal and legal future should our house be completely destroyed. For us this is not a remote possibility. We live only three blocks from the Atlantic Ocean.

In this box you should keep an envelope with the records you'll need to prove you haven't been "disappeared" by some secret agency: birth and marriage certificates, passports, insurance papers, bank books, investment records, wills, medical documents, vaccination records for children/pets, any other legal papers, and leave space for the address book and other truly last-minute items. (See the complete Disaster Supply Kit list on pages 41–42.) You should include photocopies of some recent utility bills—electric, phone, water, etc.—so you can contact these utilities with your account numbers. (Just because your house is gone doesn't mean they'll stop sending you bills.) The box should also contain a set of your phone directories in case you need to make calls to local businesses before you can return. We regularly burn complete computer back-ups onto CDs, so these would be added at the last minute; however, a laptop will fit in the box too. We also keep that single-burner butane stove in the box with some extra fuel. Because we conduct our business with computers, we would reserve car space for the CPUs, if not the monitors, as well as for our two cats, Garamond and Helvetica (not their real names).

> ## Computer Users
>
> Back up your hard disk regularly, but make a special backup if you have warning of a coming calamity. Store the disk or CD with your Disaster Supply Kit.

Unless you are escaping to the home of a relative or to a public shelter, or can afford to eat all your meals in restaurants, you may also want to bring another container. In this one you will place some nonperishable foods and a saucepan (also see The Five-Day Grocery List on page 62). You can also toss into the box some dehydrated foods (see For the Truly Lazy on page 68), as reconstituting your lasagne or minestrone soup with some boiling water will immeasurably enhance your five-day layover at Motel 6. You'll also want to bring toys for the youngsters along with some clothes and other things listed in Create a Family Plan on page 44.

Disaster Supply Kit

Whenever you are forced to leave your home, take with you as many items on this list as you can.

- Water—at least one gallon daily per person for three to seven days
- Food—enough for three to seven days; nonperishable or canned

food/juices; foods for infants or the elderly; snack food
- Cooking tools, butane stove, nonelectric can opener, fuel, paper plates, plastic utensils
- Blankets, pillows, etc.
- Clothing—seasonal, rain gear, sturdy shoes
- First-aid kit, medicines, prescription drugs
- Special items for babies and the elderly
- Toiletries such as hygiene items, moisture wipes
- Flashlight and batteries
- Radio—battery operated and National Oceanic Atmospheric Association (NOAA) weather radio
- Cash (banks and ATMs may not be open or available for extended periods)
- Keys
- Toys, books, and games
- Important documents—keep insurance, medical records, bank account numbers, social security cards, etc., in a waterproof container
- Tools (keep a set with you during the storm)
- Pet care items—proper identification, immunization records, medications; ample supply of food and water; a carrier or cage; muzzle and leash

(Courtesy of the National Hurricane Center of the National Weather Service)

Make sure your vehicle's fuel tank is filled.

For our cats, we would also bring toys, treats, a litter box, litter, and some plastic bags and a scoop, so they can maintain their self-esteem.

For information on ways in which you can strengthen your home for resistance to damage in violent storms, visit the National Hurricane Center's Web site, www.nhc.noaa.gov/HAW2/english/intro.shtml.

Riding It Out

If the authorities have not requested or ordered you to leave your home, or if you just want to try your luck, then you may elect to ride out the event inside your house. If you do, you can take steps to keep safe and guarantee some basic comforts to get you through the aftermath without becoming a manic Valkyrie who flies off the handle over the slightest thing. (This presumes that you aren't one already.)

Let's look at what the National Weather Service advises. They suggest that every household come up with a Family Disaster Plan (the sopping wet residents of Florida and North Carolina's Outer Banks are well acquainted with this). Here you assess the vulnerability of your home, retrofit your house for safety, and make sure everyone knows the procedure once all hell breaks loose.

Create a Family Plan

- Discuss the type of hazards that could affect your family
- Know your home's vulnerabilities to storm surge, flooding, and wind
- Locate a safe room or the safest areas in your home for each hurricane hazard
- Determine escape routes from your home, and places to meet
- Have an out-of-state friend as a family contact, so all your family members have a single point of contact
- Make a plan for what to do with your pets if you need to evacuate
- Post emergency telephone numbers by your phones and make sure your children know how to call 911
- Check your insurance coverage—flood damage is not usually covered by homeowners' insurance
- Stock nonperishable emergency supplies and a Disaster Supply Kit
- Use a NOAA weather radio. Remember to replace its battery every six months
- Take first-aid, CPR, and disaster preparedness classes

(Courtesy of the National Hurricane Center of the National Weather Service)

After you have meticulously fulfilled the National Weather Service (NWS) checklist, you will be as prepared as possible to weather the storm. Tucked securely in your safe room—a protected spot away from any windows—you will keep your Disaster Supply Kit nearby, grit your teeth, and wait it out. Unless the hurricane stalls over your house—and it can—it usually passes over and out of the picture in several hours. Once it's gone you will venture outside; that is, if you aren't already there. Even if you are not injured, if your house is wrecked, you may be deeply sorry you didn't evacuate. All services will be out—electricity, possibly the water supply, fire services, ambulance, police, and phones. In this situation you must be extra careful not to hurt yourself. Stay off the roof. Don't walk around barefoot. Be cautious with knives and other sharp objects.

Got Gas?

If the power goes out, gasoline may not be available. Therefore, it's a good idea to fill up your car's tank prior to any approaching storm.

But if all you've lost is your electrical power, you will start looking for another kit, one that the NWS doesn't worry about—your Five-Day Wine Box supply kit, which will contain the items you need for cooking meals that not only taste great—and with a minimum of effort—but relieve the monotony of living life in the style of Lewis and Clark. In our family-disaster-preparedness meeting, we made sure everyone knew the location of the olive oil and dried chiles.

Making Fire

Your primary necessity for eating well without power is having a reliable, efficient source of heat for emergency cooking. If you have neither working natural gas appliances nor an electrical generator, you'll want to consider the following advice for buying an inexpensive alternative source of heat. (If you're happy eating cold stew out of a can, proceed to Chapter 11.)

Camping Stoves

You can purchase a small, efficient, inexpensive emergency stove from your local camping supplies store. Did you know that for about $50 you can have a tiny little stove and a canister of fuel that will last two days? For $80 you can practically open a backyard restaurant with takeout. Camp stoves are great but made mostly for the adventurer. You may never have to reconstitute a dehydrated dinner while clinging to the side of Mt. Everest or while kayaking the North Sea, but if you pay a call to your nearest sporting-goods chain or outfitter, you will discover an amazing array of portable cookstoves for the outdoors. Some of these stoves are little more than a tiny nozzle and frame that sit atop a

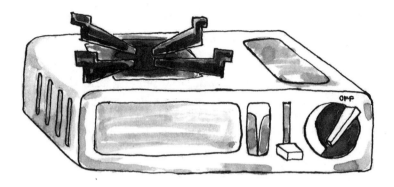

canister of fuel, but you will also find the good ole reliable Coleman two-burner stove. (Coleman even makes a folding camp oven!)

Surplus Heaven

Whether you have an emergency or not, you will enjoy hours of entertainment simply reading the Major Surplus & Survival supply catalog. They carry everything from antimicrobial socks to bush machetes and tactical gear. But they also carry MREs; survival kits, including a thirty-six-hundred-calorie emergency high energy bar that provides three days' worth of nutrients; and even a portable, non-electric washing machine that washes five-pound loads. How about a propane-fired hot shower? Go to www.majorsurplusnsurvival.com now and get on their mailing list.

For general home-based cooking, we recommend a single-burner butane unit that chefs use for demonstrations. The recipes in *Apocalypse Chow!* were tested on a Glowmaster portable butane stove, 7,000 BTU, available at www.gourmet.org and elsewhere. Similar stoves include the Burton stove, 8,400 BTU (at www.cooking.com), and the Glomate stove, 7,500 BTU (at www.glomate.com), which are designed for both indoor and outdoor use. You can also use these stoves for camping, tailgating, boating, backyard barbecues, or for cooking during emergency power outages. The stoves come with hard-sided carrying cases and cost $50–$100. Fuel canisters are inexpensive and can be purchased by the case. (See the Resources Directory on page 234 for more information.)

Bathtub Wisdom

With a big storm approaching, fill your bathtub with water. That way, if municipal water shuts off, you can still wash dishes, wash yourself, and flush the toilet. Studies show that you will desire at least two out of three of these conveniences.

Gas Grills

Another reliable heat source for cooking during an emergency is a gas grill. A patio barbecue grill will do nicely, provided that you have plenty of fuel.

It's a good idea to buy an extra cylinder of propane before a big hurricane strikes, because the roads may be impassable for days. If the emergency is merely a blackout, for which you would have no warning, you shouldn't have trouble buying a tank of fuel anytime you need it. The downside to relying on the patio grill for all your cooking is that it can only be used outdoors. This is okay if it's warm and sunny but not too practical when it's cold, raining, or snowing outside, or when you just want to make a hot cup of tea before bed. (Never use a gas grill inside your home or garage.)

Wood Fires

If you happen to have a wood-burning stove that allows you to cook on top of it, you can get by with this, as long as you have plenty of wood that can last several days. If you're only using an open campfire, however, problems abound. It takes time to build a wood fire, and once started it doesn't heat food uniformly and much of the fuel goes up in smoke. Whether you're outside or using an indoor fireplace, you will need to rig a way to heat a pot over the flames, so your pots and pans must have handles that won't melt or burn. Whenever you build a fire, use extreme caution. You would bring beaucoup heartache upon yourself if you burned down the neighborhood that had miraculously survived the hurricane.

There is one advantage to foods cooked over a wood fire, in case you just aren't able to stifle the opportunistic entrepreneur you became before Mother Nature put you in the same boat with everyone else. If you cook on the wood fire, you can sell tapas to your down-and-out neighbors. You can charge triple for flame-grilled fare, like the trendy restaurants do. (Be sure to check whether the police have ordered price gougers to be shot on sight.)

Charcoal Grills

Charcoal is as impractical and inefficient for cooking as a wood fire. When you build a substantial enough charcoal fire for cooking, the charcoal will continue to burn long after you have eaten. You can't conserve charcoal very well or, of course, use it again. If you do use charcoal for boiling water, place a saucepan with the lid on the grill and close the cover, if possible. Make sure you use a pan with handles that won't melt or catch fire. Grilling would be done as you do on the Fourth of July, but if the disaster continues on for several days, unless you have a garage full of dry charcoal, you'll be out of fuel and out of luck in short order.

About Generators

Most gasoline-powered electric generators don't produce enough juice to operate your electric range. A small 5,000-watt generator will allow you to run the fridge, lights, and perhaps some small appliances.

Other Ways to Cook

If you foolishly ignored the authorities or, worse, neglected to buy this book in time and you've found yourself in a disaster or blackout unprepared, you aren't completely out of luck. With some Sterno (canned heat) or a chafing dish, you may not be able to boil enough water for pasta, but you will be able to warm up some soup. You can always heat a pan with a kitchen or plumber's torch, or heat cans of food on the manifold of your car engine. This may not be as stupid as it sounds, once you realize that Chris Maynard and Bill Scheller wrote an entire cookbook, titled *Manifold Destiny: The One! The Only! Guide to Cooking on Your Car Engine,* for the new "mechanic's cuisine." As tempting as it might be, we don't recommend using signal flares for cooking.

In case you aren't smart enough to figure this out on your own, you should never burn charcoal inside your house. You also want to use the utmost caution when using an open flame indoors. Whenever possible, take your stove outside and do your cooking in the great outdoors. Also, never use candles indoors for light. Instead, use a bona fide camping light or a safe oil lamp or battery-operated lights. I'm not going to mention this again.

- Place candles and oil lamps safely away from flammable materials
- Keep children away from matches and open flames
- Keep an ABC (general purpose) fire extinguisher in your home
- Clear your cooking area of clutter
- Keep fittings and nozzles on bottled gas appliances clean
- Store bottled gas and other fuels away from heat sources
- Whenever cooking over open flames, be sure the cooking space is well ventilated

Other Equipment You'll Wish You Had

If you live in an area that's prone to disaster, you have to face the inexorable possibility that you may one day have to get along without your blender, coffee grinder, or microwave. That's right, you may have to prepare meals from scratch, without tools that whir, chop, or go *buzz* in the night. If this prospect seems absurd to you, counseling is recommended (it worked for us). And it's never too soon to start.

In the meantime we have blazed a new trail through the frontier of cooking without electric appliances and come up with a list of tools that will still enable you to cook fabulous meals. Be sure that somewhere in your kitchen, or at least in the attic, you have a frying pan and saucepan with metal handles. You will also want to have a food mill for pureeing by hand and a box grater for shredding and, of course, grating. A mandoline can help you make perfect slices. Whatever you use, be careful not to cut yourself, as the rescue squad may not be able to reach you. (See Indispensable Kitchen Tools below for equipment that can help you cook great meals without electricity.)

In the next chapter you will find enlightenment on what to keep in your pantry, an effective strategy for using up the food you have on hand, and how to improvise.

Indispensable Kitchen Tools

In addition to pots, pans, and sharp knives, the items on this list will help keep your kitchen humming:

- box grater
- can opener (manual)
- food mill
- garlic press
- mandoline
- mezzaluna
- mortar and pestle

- nut grinder (hand crank)
- pastry blender
- potato masher
- potato ricer
- strainers and sieves
- sudare (for sushi-making)
- vegetable chopper (manual)
- vegetable peeler
- whisks
- zester

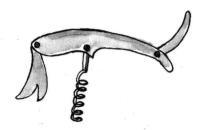

Helping Your Pets

When you plan your evacuation strategy, don't forget your pet! Bring pets indoors well in advance of a storm. Reassure them and remain calm. If you can't keep your pet with you, specialized pet shelters, animal-control shelters, veterinary clinics, and friends and relatives out of harm's way are potential refuges for your pet during a disaster.

Animals brought to a pet shelter are required to have an identification collar and rabies tag, proper identification on all belongings, a carrier or cage, a leash, an ample supply of food, water and food bowls, any necessary medications, specific care instructions, and newspapers or trash bags for cleanup. Pet shelters will be filled on a first come, first served basis. Call ahead to determine availability.

(From the Web site of The National Weather Service:

www.nhc.noaa.gov/HAW2/english/prepare/pet_plan.shtml)

Get Ready

Visit www.ready.gov, the U.S. Department of Homeland Security's Web site for advice on natural disasters; planning kits; and all your explosion, biological-threat, chemical-threat, nuclear-blast, and radiation needs.

Chapter 3

The Well-Tempered Pantry

Regardless of the reason, when the electricity goes out, cooking a decent meal becomes a challenge. If they don't turn off the gas, your gas range will still work. With an electrical generator, you can run your fridge, but it would take a mighty generator to amp up your electric range. Without a generator, however, once the power goes off, that ominously silent refrigerator will steadily turn your frozen and chilled foods into Dumpster fodder. What you need now is a food supply that doesn't require refrigeration. In this chapter *Apocalypse Chow!* gives you the Well-Tempered Pantry along with some skookum tricks that can put food on the table no matter what.

Stock Options

You can beat Mother Nature at her own game by hoarding a secret stash of versatile, nonperishable foods that store at room temperature.

The type of power outage you're preparing for will help determine how much food to buy. If you live in Chicago, odds are you'll never get hit with a hurricane. If you're squirreling away enough provender to get through a thunderstorm, you'll need a smaller pantry stash than someone who is hedging his bet against Hurricane Zoe or even the apocalypse itself. Another factor is the number of people in your household. If it's just one or two of you, for example, buy small cans of, say, canned green beans and leave the buying-club industrial-size skid to the Brady Bunch down the street. Before you make your shopping list, it will also be helpful to have menu ideas of what you'll want to eat when you enter the lightless abyss. It makes no sense to buy a dozen cans of beets if everyone else hates them. That's a lot of borscht to eat all by yourself.

Fortunately for you *Apocalypse Chow!* takes the guesswork out of this process by providing suggested menus and a grocery list to get you and up to three companions through five days with pretty good food.

> ### "Abandon Ship" Rations
>
> Take a tip from the U.S. Navy, whose "Abandon Ship" rations could save your life when the water rises or if another one of those Noah events rolls in. Check it out at www.dscp.dla.mil/subs/rations/programs/survival/shipabt.htm. This ration will last one person for three days. It's a well-thought-out model for your own "abandon ship" scenario.

Making Your List

The following sections provide concise ideas for short- or long-term food lists along with suggestions that can make the difference between merely surviving and really living. At the end of this chapter is the Well-Tempered Pantry list—a roster of foods and other items you really ought to stock up on before the next disaster.

Now I must confess that I get easily confused by long complicated lists. My eyes glaze over. My left brain goes on vacation. So in order to make this simpler for all of us, I begged the Divine Forces of the Universe to show me an easier way.

The Five-Day Wine Box

My strategy for making this book easy to use required that I dumb down Robin's expert advice on nonperishable foods, her amazingly quick recipes, and what to have in the house, so that even I could understand it. One day when she wasn't home I conducted an experiment in her kitchen, an act that is not without its risks.

The Well-Tempered Pantry list looked to me like something the Pentagon might request for spreading freedom in a foreign country, so I picked just enough recipes to make lunches and dinners for up to four people for five days, and then consolidated the lists. In my experiment I picked out the items in what had been Robin's well-organized pantry, and then went shopping for the rest, visiting each aisle in the Harris Teeter three or four times, as I was unfamiliar with that bewildering terrain.

The total cost was about fifty dollars. That's not bad to get a family of four, or four neighborhood reprobates, through five days without electricity. Once I assembled all the goods on the kitchen table, I looked around for a box to hold it all and discovered that it would all fit neatly into a single empty wine carton (I chose a Chateau Ste. Michelle, 2003 Pinot Gris, which holds twelve one-liter bottles). The Five-Day Wine Box works out great because it doesn't take up much room. Since the goodies are nonperishable, this box can hide in the bottom of a linen closet, the basement, the galley of a boat, a dorm room, or in any other out-of-the-way corner. (While I think a wine box is ideal because of its size, you may instead prefer to use a plastic tub with a lid, as it would be waterproof, larger, and frustrate vermin.)

As you look over the following menus, be aware that this list reflects our own personal likes and dislikes. For your menus you can flip through the book and choose the recipes you prefer. You can also fill more boxes, for more people, for more days, or because you are obsessive-compulsive, paranoid, or both. Remember that the menus provide recipes for basic, well-balanced, one-dish meals, but without any extras, side dishes, or desserts. Also keep in mind that without refrigeration, you can't create leftovers; so if you are a couple or a single person, plan accordingly. Here are the recipes I chose, followed by the grocery list of items you'll need from the store to make them.

The Five-Day Menu

Day One

Lunch

Comforting Corn Chowder

Beat-the-Blahs Basic Black Bean Patties

Dinner

Red Rum Chili

Day Two

Lunch

"Seeing Stars" White Beans and Greens Soup

Dinner

Kitchen Sink Capellini

Day Three

Lunch

"We're Not in Provence Anymore" *Salade Nicoise*

Dinner

Curry in a Hurry

Day Four

Lunch

Composed Marinated Vegetable Salad

Texas Twister Caviar

Dinner

Orecchiette with White Beans and Olivada

Day Five

Lunch

Calm-Down Couscous Salad

Dinner

"Duck and Cover" Tortilla Bake

The Five-Day Grocery List

Three 15.5-ounce cans kidney beans

One 15.5-ounce can black beans

One 15.5-ounce can pinto beans

One 8-ounce can chickpeas

One 15.5-ounce can chickpeas

One 16-ounce can cannellini beans

One 15.5-ounce can white beans

One 15.5-ounce can black-eyed peas

Four 14.5-ounce cans diced tomatoes

One 28-ounce can diced tomatoes

One 15-ounce can crushed tomatoes

One 15-ounce can corn

One 15-ounce can creamed corn

One 8-ounce can sliced white potatoes

Four 16-ounce cans diced white potatoes

One 8-ounce can spinach

One 8-ounce can green beans

Two 15-ounce cans green beans

Two 16-ounce jars three-bean salad

Two 15-ounce cans vegetable broth

Three 4-ounce cans chopped mild green chiles

One 8-ounce jar cured black olives

One 8-ounce jar kalamata olives

One 4-ounce can sliced black olives

One 6-ounce jar marinated artichoke hearts

One 16-ounce jar salsa

One 8-ounce jar roasted red bell peppers

One package shelf-stable tortillas

One pound orecchiette

One pound capellini
One box whole-grain couscous
One box soup pasta (pastene, stellini, etc.)
One 8-ounce carton soy milk
One container bread crumbs

Note: For add-ons to enjoy with this menu (such as tortilla chips with the chili, crackers with the Texas Twister Caviar, or caponata or giardiniera salad with the pasta dishes) see Supply List for Box #2.

These meals will get you through the first five days in fine style, but in the meantime, you need to know about what's not included in your box, so you don't find yourself discovering on Day One that you have stranded yourself without necessities such as cheese puffs, pecan sandies, and margarita mix.

Not included in the Five-Day Wine Box are kitchen utensils, breakfast items, prepackaged snacks, desserts, beverages, or recipe accompaniments such as crackers, bread, or other items to round out the meals.

You can do breakfast easily with boxed and instant cereals, pancake mix, cereal bars, milk or soy milk, and bread. As your butter or margarine won't last very long, you'll also want to have a jar of peanut butter (think "extra protein"), some jam, and instant coffee (or ground coffee if you have a French press) or tea bags. Our emergency breakfast usually consists of instant oatmeal or cold cereal, toast with peanut butter, and coffee. For the cereal we use soy milk from small aseptic containers. If you drink dairy, you can mix powdered milk with water. To make toast we just hold a piece of bread over the butane flame with long metal kitchen tongs.

What, No Coffeemaker?

For my money, a French-press coffeemaker does a great job when the juice isn't flowing. It's fun to use and looks cool, too. If retro is more your style, consider one of those stove-top aluminum jobs with the little glass knob that shows the coffee is percolating. You can also go the "cowboy way" by boiling water with ground coffee in a saucepan over a flame, then pouring it (through a strainer, please) into a mug.

Also not included in the Five-Day Wine Box are cooking oil and spices, which you probably already have. There's enough space in the box for some powdered milk, a small bottle of cooking oil, and some little spice bottles, etc. Here, then, is the not-included-in-the-Five-Day-Wine-Box list, or, as I like to think of it, a list of stuff for Box #2. It's a great box to have around for evacuation, or if you'll be cooking away from home, whether for college or camping. It's also ideal for helpless bachelors and other singles. Remember that nonperishable food won't spoil, waiting for you to get around to cooking it.

Supply List for Box #2

To make the recipes in the Five-Day Menu, you will want these spices and add-ons. Since you probably already have the spices in your house, consider assembling small plastic sandwich bags of the spices you will need to put with your supplies in the event an evacuation becomes necessary. Suggested add-ons are included at the end of this list, though you can customize this list to suit your tastes. Include breakfast items, snacks, and beverages in this box as well.

basil	cayenne pepper
chili powder	chives
curry powder	garlic
lemon juice	marjoram
minced onion	mustard
olive oil	oregano
parsley	pine nuts
red pepper flakes	sage
salt	sun-dried tomatoes
savory	pepper
vegetable bouillon cubes	slivered almonds
capers	vinegar

Recipe add-ons: crackers and other bread items (for soups, salads, etc.), giardiniera salad and caponata (for the pasta dishes), papadums (for the curry), tortilla chips (for the chili)

Breakfast items: cereals, breakfast bars, peanut butter, etc.

Snacks and desserts: canned fruit, cookies, nuts, energy bars, trail mix

Beverages: coffee, tea, juice, milk or soy milk, etc.

Just-in-case items: If you have room in the box, toss in a couple jars of pasta sauce and a few boxes of pasta. Maybe stash a few bricks of ramen noodles, too . . . just in case.

Note: You can also prepare a Box #3 in which you can assemble general kitchen items, dishwashing soap and basins, skillet, saucepan, and, of course, your portable stove. If you're cooking at home, most of this stuff will already be in place. However, in the event of evacuation, having everything in one place will come in handy.

For the Truly Lazy

We're confident that the recipes in *Apocalypse Chow!* will see you serenely through most emergency mealtime situations in fifteen minutes or less. However, there may be occasions when you just don't feel like cooking, no matter how simple the recipe. For those times when opening a can of tomatoes would siphon your last ERG, do not fear, for we, who can reach this nadir of endurance even on a good day, have options for you. Good options.

MREs

You can always squirrel away some "retort foods." Otherwise known as MREs (Meals Ready to Eat), these individual meals are sealed in "retort packaging," tough laminated aluminum pouches that can be stored unrefrigerated for months. Military-style MREs will last unrefrigerated for as long as thirty months when stored at 90 degrees—longer at lower temperatures. You will want to be aware that MREs are expensive.

Sometimes scoffed at as "Meals Rejected by Ethiopians" by soldiers in the field, government issue–style MREs are not dehydrated. They are ready to eat cold from the package. You can warm the package in boiling water, on a car engine, or with a flameless heater (a small slab that heats up when you add water). You can obtain flameless heaters from www.heatermeals.com

as well as from other Web sites and camping supply stores.

These military MREs are available to consumers, too, but without the government insignia and warnings printed on the package. Please note that the MREs marked for government use are illegal for you to buy or even possess. ("I served nine years for possessing a small amount of manicotti with vegetables for personal use. Can you spare some change to help me get back on my feet?")

The legal ones are available online (see Resources Directory) and in some stores. Be on the alert for stolen GI food and report scofflaws to the proper authorities. However tempted you may be, avoid buying illegal MREs at the next gun show you attend. Also be sure to avoid any supplier offering used MREs.

Food Storage Tips for the Pessimist

This food list is intended for long-term survival. According to the Federal Emergency Management Agency (FEMA), these are the amounts of food you should store for one person for one month. One can survive for years on small daily amounts of these items.

- Wheat—twenty pounds
- Corn—twenty pounds
- Powdered milk (for babies and infants)—twenty pounds (should be purchased in nitrogen-packed cans)
- Soybeans—ten pounds
- Iodized salt—one pound
- Vitamin C pills—fifteen grams (vitamins should be rotated every two years)

(Courtesy of the Federal Emergency Management Agency. See more at

www.fema.gov/library/emfdwtr.shtm)

Freeze-Dried Meals

Similar to MREs are freeze-dried meals. They too come in pouches, but require hot water to reconstitute them. Extremely lightweight, these foods are a favorite with backpackers, campers, and other outdoorspersons. They can be found in most sporting-goods and outfitters stores, and offer astonishing variety. With prepared meals ranging from seafood chowder to beef teriyaki and blueberry cheesecake, it's an insidious temptation to stock up. We were particularly intrigued since many of the brands offer a good selection of vegetarian entrées, including Wild-Rice-and-Mushroom Pilaf, Pasta Primavera, and Black-Bean-and-Rice Burritos. We tested three different varieties and found them to be improbably tasty. Freeze-dried meals can usually last for years if stored in cool temperatures.

You'll want to know the downsides of using these prepared meals. First is the cost. At $3 to $6 per serving, buying enough to feed a family of four for a week can be irrefragably expensive, though still cheaper than dining in a restaurant was when the restaurants were open. (You may miss the ambience, but not the sneering goth waitress.) You can check out the pre-assembled kits of these meals online. Try the Just in Case unit by Mountain House. It contains enough food to feed one person for seven days. (Visit www.mountainhouse.com for current prices.) Another drawback to both MREs and freeze-dried meals is the flagrant menu exclusions: Don't bother looking for pissaladiere, waterzooi, or even cuitlachoche for you corn-smut aficionados out there. They don't have a mangetout gratin or an Indonesian rijsttafel, either. I checked. (The hypothesis of a Minute Rijsttafel has yet to be tested by independent kitchen laboratories.)

For large families for the short- or long-term preparedness in general, you can also get emergency foods in restaurant-size #10 cans. Because the moisture has been removed, they are lightweight and easy to store at room temperature. These include fully prepared items, such as stews, spaghetti with sauce, raspberry crumble, or individual side dishes such as peas, corn, or rice that you can scoop out and rehydrate as needed. Again, buy sizes that you can consume in one sitting.

With ready-to-eat meals of either kind, you're paying for the convenience, but you might consider splurging on just a few to break up the routine from cooking. A dozen packets wouldn't take up much room to store until that rainy day and could even live in your Five-Day Wine Box until needed.

Even with your Five-Day Wine Box, you may want MREs for another reason.

"I'm too depressed to even boil water," you whine. Well, if the kids are old enough, with MREs you can let them cook.

"Bobby and Maryann. Stop fighting and warm up the MREs."

Keeping spare survival meals in the house can be a secret weapon if you have fussy family members. For example, if you and your spouse are in the mood to make your own spicy Thai or Indian food one night and your child is tossing his room because he wants French fries, you can appease the little squirt by adding water to a pouch of freeze-dried macaroni and cheese. Child stifled. Case closed.

You can also keep your kids involved with some freeze-dried astronaut food—located near the MREs wherever fine MREs are sold. If your kids are little, or just not too bright, you can pretend you're ordering takeout from Mars. The fact is, in addition to full meals you can find freeze-dried ice-cream sandwiches, fruit, and even gummy worms. (You can buy gummy worms by the case, by the skid, or by the truckload, depending on the tastes of your family.) While we're on the topic of astronaut food, you can also send your kids into orbit with a jar of Tang to wash down those gummy worms. (Tang mix, of course, keeps without refrigeration.)

A wide variety of MREs and freeze-dried foods can be purchased online at many Web sites. See the Resources Directory for a partial list.

Water, Water Everywhere . . .

Plan on one gallon of water per person per day for drinking, cooking, and brushing teeth. Be sure to allow water for pets, too. If you have to rely on rainwater, or water from a creek or lake, make it bacterially safe by boiling it for two minutes.

SREs

If you're like us, your trips to the supermarket rarely, if ever, include a trip down the packaged-foods aisle—you know, the one with the boxed "helpers" and packages of Day-Glo orange macaroni. Until we needed to load in supplies for hurricanes, the canned-soup section was as esoteric to us as, well, canned soup. We now regard such prepared foods with a disquieting respect. We figure as long as we have to eat pantry food, it should at least be as homemade as possible with as few preservatives, additives, and other ingredients we may not like. (What's your guess that a box that says "Italian-flavored" won't taste like it was prepared tableside by Mario Batali?)

Sure, you could get by with prepared canned foods—but who wants to eat canned spaghetti rings for even one meal, much less five meals straight? When the power's out, we prefer to put together our own soups, stews, and pasta dishes, albeit from canned ingredients, but at least we've prepared them according to our own taste, not someone named Campbell, Boyardee, or Dinty. Besides, it gives you a feeling that you have *control* over something, even if it's just how much basil or hot sauce to add to the soup. I say prepare your own dishes with the recipes in *Apocalypse Chow!* Adjust those seasonings and ingredients according to your own taste and preference. Be creative!

We've gradually come to realize that there is a place for a judicious amount of what we call "Supermarket Ready to Eats" (SREs). A few well-chosen SREs can serve to ease the workload of making dinner on an especially taxing day, to satisfy fussy eaters in your family, and to break up the routine. When you shop for SREs, be ready to read the fine print. If there's more than one or two words long enough to sabotage a Scrabble game, then you might want to return to the safety of your pantry. Here are some examples of what we call SREs.

Supermarket

Supermarkets carry a variety of instant and ready-to-eat meals in pouches, cans, boxes, and jars. Some of these products are heat-and-serve, while others require boiling water to reconstitute them. They're easy, economical, and a practical alternative when you don't feel like cooking.

Soups—available and ready-to-eat in cans, jars, and aseptic boxes as well as dehydrated in just-add-water envelopes and cups. Soups of every description are available, including tortilla soup, borscht, and the ubiquitous ramen noodle soups

Stews—packaged similarly to soups. Varieties include canned chili, Brunswick stew, and other hearty meals

Pilafs—a wide range of rice, couscous, and other grain pilafs in a variety of flavors, including Cajun style, Italian, and others. There are also mixes for risotto, tabbouleh, falafel, potato pancakes, kasha, and matzo balls

Macaroni and cheese—dozens of styles are available from boxed Day-Glo orange to organic, also in cans and individual serving cups. Spin-offs include just-add-water pasta dishes in envelopes and boxes. Also "helper" type products

Specialty foods—We found canned Hoppin' John, squash casserole, green-bean casserole, potatoes au gratin, and other savory side dishes. Also, chowchow, three-bean salad, and more

The cognoscente should brace for a shock. To be ready for the next Big Dark, you would be well-advised to sneak a small supply of instant packaged mixes into your home. That's right, Minute Rice, Rice-A-Roni (the San Francisco treat), instant oatmeal, instant mashed potatoes, a few dozen envelopes of instant soups, and that incestuous family of boxed helpers that contain pasta, potatoes, or rice; dehydrated vegetables; and various sauces. (Just add "meat," which can be anything from a can of beans, to textured vegetable protein (TVP), to tuna fish or diced Spam.)

Before you cast this book down in horror, you must bow to the inevitable necessity of using these products when the power is off. It's all about using your fuel judiciously. So you won't need therapy later, dip herewith into a tureen of wisdom and repeat one of these phrases, "I am making this sacrifice for the common good," "I have chosen to wear the mantle of family 'hero' (or 'heroine')," or "I am the culinary martyr of the household, and y'all owe me a huge debt of gratitude."

If it makes you feel better, hire a discreet shopping service to bring these instant products home, or pack them into a briefcase so you can sneak them from your car to your back door.

Keep in mind that many of these packaged meals are high in sodium and contain additives and preservatives, but again, one or two might come in handy in a pinch. For the scientifically minded, you can always buy yourself a dehydrator and package your own dehydrated meals. (See Do-It-Yourself Food Dehydration on page 78.)

Do-It-Yourself Food Dehydration

If putting together your own supply of fully prepared meals appeals to you, consider investing in a food dehydrator. Roughly the size of a large microwave oven, a dehydrator can set you back a couple of hundred bucks, but it can save money in the long run if you use it regularly.

Food dehydration is "in" as of late, thanks to backpacking and raw-food enthusiasts. In dehydration the water is slowly removed, and the food becomes lightweight and shelf-stable, thus making it ideal for emergency provisions. You can dehydrate any type of meal, such as spaghetti and meatballs, soups, and stews; snacks and sides, including crackers, breads, vegetable chips, fruit leather, cookies; and a host of other creations for convenience and high nutrition. During your day-to-day cooking routine, just double the recipes—serve one meal for dinner and dehydrate the other for emergencies.

It's a great way to prepare fresh produce for future enjoyment without losing a lot of the nutrients.

Going Native

If your taste buds sometimes walk on the wild side, here's a great idea on how to jazz up your emergency larder: Go ethnic. Depending on where you live, there may be a Chinatown, Little Italy, or other ethnic enclave nearby where great food markets abound. In Hampton Roads, Virginia, a crossroads for many branches of the military, we have great ethnic markets including Asian, Indian, Middle Eastern, Italian, and Latin.

During the calm before a storm, schedule a field trip to the ethnic markets of your choice and roam the aisles in search of intriguing nonperishables. You are guaranteed to find some items that sound tempting or that at least pique your culinary curiosity. Often these items are less pricey than you will find in a gourmet market or even at a common grocery store. In an Asian market you might find wasabi peas, canned straw mushrooms, and Thai curry mix. An Italian market could yield instant polenta, small jars of cured olives, marinated vegetable salads, and canned San Marzano tomatoes. Here is a partial list of the great food finds we discovered on our last mad shopping trip.

Indian

Favorites: We love the delicious protein-rich snack food such as a seven-ounce bag of dal-stuffed samosas. They're crunchy, spicy, and addictive. We also like the roasted chickpeas. You'll be stunned by the variety.

assorted vegetable and fruit chutneys
basmati rice pilaf mixes
golden fried onions
instant dosa mix (pancakes)
khari biscuits and other various breads
panchrattan (potato and dried fruit mix)
roasted channa (chickpeas)
samosa snacks (stuffed w/dal, cashews, raisins, and spices)
soya wadi (dehydrated soy chunks)
various pickled vegetables

Middle Eastern

Favorites: Falafel mix (just add water) forms protein-rich veggie burgers. They're a great main dish. You can also shape falafel into small balls and fry them as a snack. The canned dolmas are almost as good as homemade.

bulgur
canned fava beans (ful medames)
dolmas
dried shallots and shallot powder
falafel mix
fried eggplant slices
pistachios
pita breads
sesame crunch
stuffed cabbage

Latin

Favorites: Plantain chips are a yummy snack, and small cans of guava nectar make a nice change from OJ. You'll find a good variety of canned beans and salsas. We especially enjoy the black refried beans served with plantain chips.

canned beans of all kinds
canned breadfruit nuts
guanabana (custard apple) nectar
guava spread
pickled cabbage
plantain chips
refried pintos and refried black beans
salsas in a variety of flavors and sizes
West Indian callaloo (a native garden vegetable)
zucchini flowers

Asian

Favorites: Canned or jarred wheat gluten is an easy way to get tasty, chewy protein. It can be cut and stir-fried or added to soups and stews. We also love the variety of canned mushrooms and roasted chestnuts at ninety-nine cents a bag.

boil-in-bags (curried vegetables and other flavors)
canned mushrooms such as oyster, golden needle, and straw
dried kanpyo (gourd strips)
noodle soups (ramen and beyond)
pickled vegetables (assorted)
preserved yam candies (Asian gummy bears)
roasted chestnuts
taro chips
wheat gluten and vegetarian mock meats
wasabi peas

Italian

Favorites: The caponata is wonderful. The seven-ounce can is just enough for two as a snack or side dish. Caponata and other canned and jarred vegetables, such as the roasted zucchini and giardiniera, taste great as is and make quick, easy, and flavorful veggie accompaniments for pasta dishes.

caponata

fava beans

giardiniera

gnocchi

cups of instant risotto, fettuccine Alfredo, etc.

lupine beans

marinated mushrooms

roasted zucchini

sliced eggplant strips

tortellini

Following is the promised Well-Tempered Pantry list. This complete and thorough list is worth some study now, before a disaster strikes, because then it will be too late to go shopping. After a quick review it's off to Chapter 4 and some words about the thrill and mystery of pantry cooking.

The Well-Tempered Pantry

This list will provide day-to-day essential items for short-term preparedness. Use it as a guide to make a specific list of items that your family will actually eat. (Tip: If they hate canned okra now, they'll still hate it during an emergency.) On your customized list, note quantities of each item you will need to feed the number of people in your family for as long as a week.

Beverages

bottled water (one gallon per person per day)

cocoa

fruit and vegetable juices

instant coffee

juice drinks

milk or soy milk in aseptic containers

milk or soy milk, powdered

soft drinks

tea bags

wine, beer, etc.

Breakfast Foods

breakfast-cereal bars

pancake mix

ready-to-eat cereals

uncooked instant hot cereals

Comfort Foods/Snacks

canned fruit

chocolate bars

cookies

dried fruits such as raisins, currants, apricots, cranberries, apples, plums,
mangos, and pineapples
granola bars
hard candy and lollipops
nut and seed butters such as cashew butter, almond butter, peanut butter,
and sesame butter
a variety of nuts and seeds
peanut-butter crackers
ready-to-eat or instant puddings
trail mix

Grains, Pasta, and Noodles

basmati rice

buckwheat soba

bulgur

cornmeal

couscous

Cream of Wheat

wide variety of dried pasta such as angel hair, penne, and rotini

gnocchi, tortellini

instant grits

instant polenta

jasmine rice

kasha

millet

no-boil lasagna

oatmeal

quick-cooking brown and white rice

ramen

rice noodles

udon

Prepared Foods (canned, boxed, etc.)

bamboo shoots

bean sprouts

wide variety of canned beans such as chickpeas, cannellini, pintos, black, fava, and kidney (Note: dried beans require long cooking times, and there-fore consume too much fuel.)

a variety of fruits

pickled vegetables

stews and chili

salads such as three bean and caponata

refried beans

cans, boxes, packets, or cups of instant soup

silken tofu in aseptic packages
tomatillos
tomato products such as puree, sauce, diced, whole, and paste
TVP in a variety of sizes and flavors such as granules, nuggets, vegetable
and bean soup strips, and chicken
a variety of vegetables such as green beans, corn, spinach, potatoes,
and water chestnuts
wheat gluten (seitan)

Breads and Crackers

assorted crackers
bread products such as bread sticks
canned brown bread
taco shells
tortillas

Cooking Sauces and Other Liquids

barbecue sauce
canola, olive, and sesame oils
canned coconut milk
cooking wines such as marsala, sherry, dry red, and dry white
lemon and lime juices in small plastic containers

pasta sauces

tamari sauce

teriyaki sauce

balsamic and other flavored vinegars

Flavor makers

canned artichoke bottoms

marinated artichoke hearts

roasted bell peppers in jars

black pepper

capers

crushed red pepper flakes

crystallized ginger

curry powder

dried mushrooms such as shiitake, cremini, and porcini

dried spices such as garlic powder, onion powder, oregano, and chili powder

giardiniera salad in jars

pickled ginger

fresh bottled ginger

canned hearts of palm

iodized sea salt

maple syrup

canned mild and hot chiles

fresh onions and/or dehydrated minced onions

fresh potatoes and/or dehydrated potato flakes (Note: Fresh potatoes and
onions can be stored unrefrigerated in a cool and dry place.)

regular or soy Parmesan cheese in shaker-type containers

salsa

seasoning blends such as Mrs. Dash and Herbamere

small jars of jams and jellies

sea vegetables such as nori, dulse, and wakame for high nutrition

sugar

dehydrated sun-dried tomatoes

Tabasco

tapenade

vegetable bouillon cubes or powdered vegetable soup base

wasabi powder

Other

aluminum foil

plastic wrap

baking powder

egg replacer powder

nonstick cooking spray

resealable food-storage bags
vitamin C tablets; multivitamins

(Note: When you customize your list, remember to add baby food, pet food, or other special foods that your family may require. And don't forget to toss in an extra copy of *Apocalypse Chow!*)

When planning your pantry, be sure to check the suppliers of nonperishable foods in the Resources Directory.

Chapter 4

Pantry Cuisine

Pantry Cuisine. Remember that you saw it here first.

There are those who wonder if your humble author merely hovers in the shadow of his celebrity-chef wife, but the truth is, I know my way around a kitchen. Don't let that morsel of information get around, lest more be expected of me in the future. However, during the years when Robin was indentured to the restaurant kitchens, I had to fend for myself. Though I didn't have her skills with food, I made creative use of the pantry—considered it my personal store from which I chose my nightly repast.

It is with that experience under my belt that I present Pantry Cuisine. Okay, Robin helped put this together. A lot. However, we regard this food as the best you can do when the refrigerator's out to lunch and nothing fresh is available. (Someone alert the food police.)

But It's Not Fresh

Robin has ingeniously designed the *Apocalypse Chow!* recipes so you can eat well through your tough days without electricity. The recipes presume that you have already eaten your fresh food and have now begun to raid the pantry. They were created for maximum flavor and nutrition using a minimum of time and fuel. Included are soups, stews, main dishes, salads, snacks, desserts, and all the meals listed in your Five-Day Wine Box, and these recipes draw on the items in your Well-Tempered Pantry.

As an added bonus most of the recipes were designed for one-pot cooking. This will make short work of both the cooking and the cleanup. In order to economize on water and fuel, some recipes will make double use of single functions. Get this: You'll find a pasta and bean recipe in which the canned beans are placed in a colander to drain, and then the cooked pasta is dumped over them, allowing the hot pasta water to heat up the beans and rinse them at the same time. (As you know, canned beans and other canned vegetables have already been cooked.)

You won't need anything fancy to make these recipes, but you will need these basics:

1. a heat source for cooking, such as a butane stove (Chapter 2)
2. a supply of ingredients from your Well-Tempered Pantry (Chapter 3)

3. some pots, pans, and cooking utensils
4. enough potable water for cooking (in addition to water for drinking and washing dishes)
5. basins for washing and rinsing, along with products to wash and sanitize dishes

Now it's time to point out the obvious: If you are accustomed to buying fresh produce, you may be horrified by our obscene and unrestrained use of canned vegetables. But desperate times call for desperate measures. Without electricity you simply won't have any choice. You will have to accept the fact that even canned vegetables are better than digging "lips and peckers" out of a tin (see *Slingblade*).

Now hear ye all adherents to the Fresh Veggie Dogma (I'm one myself)! You can take precautions to hedge your bet. Most power outages come suddenly, but if you do have notice of a possible power outage, there are some sturdy vegetables that can tolerate sitting around at room temperature for several days or longer. (Indeed you may already be storing them at room temperature.) Think onions, garlic, carrots, and other root vegetables, but don't forget to consider your precious fuel. (Sing "My Butane" to the tune of "Denke Shoen.")

Here's a perfect example: Let's say when the power goes out, you'd been saving a magnificent five-pound kabocha squash to make a glorious bisque. Now you find yourself a wreck, contemplating said squash like Rodin's *The Thinker,* and you only have one can of butane to get the job done. Face it—this is a relationship that you will simply have to put on hold. Lovingly store that seductive Japanese squash in a cool, dry place for better times and, instead, open a can of pumpkin puree. A tasty soup will be ready in minutes instead of hours, and you'll have enough fuel left over to make many more meals.

A Root Cellar

Our ancestors stored onions, garlic, potatoes, squashes, and root vegetables, such as carrots and parsnips, in a cool, dark, dry root cellar. Today's houses are more likely to have a wine cellar than a root cellar, but that doesn't mean you can't store root veggies there (or another cool, dry place). Just bear in mind that the sturdier (or harder) the vegetable, the longer it takes to cook. So, when cooking them, be aware that they will consume extra fuel.

The same goes for cooking fresh instead of dehydrated onions. You'll need to tack on an extra five minutes cooking time to soften that onion; same for carrots. If you *do* plan to use fresh onions, be sure to get small ones, because you can't have the leftover half of a large one sitting around until the next day. As an option, consider switching to shallots. These delicate beauties are small, cook up fast, and can add a touch of elegance to your pot of slumgullion. Plus, did you know that the shallot is the only member of the onion family that doesn't give you the breath from hell? (In ancient times shallots were considered an aphrodisiac. Just a guess, but it could have something to do with that breath thing.)

You can also buy some underripe bananas, avocados, pears, and tomatoes, as they can ripen unrefrigerated on the windowsill to provide fresh nutrients down the road. Citrus fruits such as oranges, grapefruit, lemons, and limes also do well at room temperature.

If you dutifully stocked your Well-Tempered Pantry, you will be prepared for cooking meals under powerless conditions. If you do have some fresh produce to incorporate into these recipes, then by all means use it while it lasts. If you have fresh herbs, feel free to substitute fresh for dried in the recipes. (Note: One teaspoon of dried = one tablespoon of fresh.) The most important thing with these recipes is to be creative and have fun modifying them.

Eat It Before It Spoils

As long as you have a heat source, whether it's a gas stove, camp stove, or outdoor gas grill, dinner is only minutes away—that is, if you take emergency cuisine to heart at the get-go. Think of it as the trendiest new cuisine, rare and exclusive, that can be practiced on specific occasions and that is beyond the reach of most people. Take pictures in case you decide to submit them to the Dining section of the *New York Times*.

The Fridge

Let us begin. Armed with the nonelectrical implements you ran out to buy immediately after reading Chapter 2, and twitching with anticipation to dig into your Well-Tempered Pantry, you'll now assess what needs to be cooked first.

Cold preserves food, whether refrigerated or frozen, but with the power out, your stored cold foods will begin to defrost and spoil. Your first meals during a power outage, therefore, will use up what's in the refrigerator followed by what's in the freezer. Use them up in this order:

1. anything that is highly perishable such as leftovers or other home-cooked foods, open containers that state "refrigerate after opening," refrigerated tofu or soy milk, and anything containing animal products

2. moderately perishable items such as leafy greens

3. items that may last longer such as firm, hard, or uncut vegetables

> ### Food Temperature Safety
>
> According to the United States Department of Agriculture (USDA), when food is stored at higher than 40 degrees Fahrenheit, bacteria can double in number every 20 minutes. This is true for raw foods as well as foods that have already been cooked. Foods in a jammed, well-insulated freezer stay frozen the longest—up to three days if the door remains closed. The presence of ice crystals in the center of food tells you that a frozen item is still safe to eat. (See Appendix on page 231.)

Since Robin and I are vegetarians, the most perishable items in our fridge prior to Hurricane Isabel were tofu and butter lettuce. For others it may be shrimp or leftover *coeur à la crème*. Be sure to dispose of anything approaching science experiment status, but also remember that when food is stored above 40 degrees Fahrenheit, bacteria doubles its number every 20 minutes. Be especially cautious—don't take chances with products that contain meat, eggs, or dairy products. As you follow this plan, only open the refrigerator and freezer doors when absolutely necessary.

Before you start using up the perishables, make a list of what you have on hand and divvy up the items into workable menus. I don't know about your fridge, but in ours at any given time you might find truffle oil, jicama, rosewater, umeboshi plums, maitake mushrooms, three kinds of tofu, fennel bulbs, and tamari. What would you make for dinner? It's fun to play the home version of *Door Knock Dinners,* made popular by Gordon Elliott on the Food Network TV show. Begin the game on your front porch. If nobody answers, let yourself in.

We remember everything that was in the fridge during the tedious wait for power after Hurricane Isabel. We had anticipated the storm, so Robin purchased only nonperishables at the supermarket that week and used up as much of the perishable good stuff in the days preceding the storm. The first day without power our refrigerator still offered a few carrots, some celery, scallions, fresh parsley, and green beans. A container of previously cooked escarole and several very ripe tomatoes from our garden were also prime candidates for the cook pot. Of course, we also had onions and garlic. So how did we fare?

The first meal after Isabel, we cooked Italian. We made a small pot of soup with the fresh vegetables, adding the cooked escarole close to serving time. The warming sustenance of homemade soup is always good for what ails you, and we reasoned that our nerves jangling from our property being hammered by ninety-mile-an-hour winds was good enough reason to savor a soothing soup.

We salvaged our bounty of nearly overripe tomatoes by turning them into a cheeky puttanesca sauce, which also allowed us to use up the remaining parsley and a partial container of imported olives that had languished on the refrigerator shelf. With no food processor we did the chopping by hand: each with a small cutting board and a couple of sharp Henkel knives, tapping our feet to the beat of the hand-crank radio. (I'll always associate "Bad Moon Rising" with Hurricane Isabel.) Making dinner took longer, of course, but we had no place to go and needed ways to fill time. An hour after enjoying the last twirl of pasta, we remembered several ripe peaches that inspired a comforting dessert. And so it was that instead of feeling sorry for ourselves, we spent our time creating a fabulous meal that would have been delicious even *with* electrical power.

Your goal is to come up with menus that are appetizing, nutritious, and easy to make—limited only by what you have on hand and your imagination. Be creative and try to incorporate a theme of some sort to tie the meal together. Successive days would be similarly planned: Canned refried beans and a jar of salsa would spell the beginnings of a zesty Mexican fiesta, while that jar of peanut butter can be transformed into a sumptuous and spicy Thai peanut sauce for noodles and canned veggies.

If you have to cook a lot of food to save it from the garbage can, go ahead and make a mountainous stir-fry. You can also grill everything in sight in a shameless cookout orgy. If all you have are small amounts of miscellaneous vegetables, prepare a beauteous soup or a bounteous stew. If you're truly well-stocked, share the wealth. Invite neighbors over. If you know of an elderly couple down the street, bring them some portions of whatever you make. They'll be thrilled for the hot meal and remember you fondly when the big mess is over.

By the second day your refrigerator should be bare of most perishable foods. Leafy produce generally wilts beyond the point of salvaging after the second day. It's okay to keep some of the condiments in there that don't spoil easily, such as soy sauce, ketchup, and mustard, and, of course, extra cans of soda and beer. But at this point you'll want to toss that opened jar of mayo or that carton of half-and-half. Ditto for the butter.

The Freezer

You used up the fridge fodder first because it spoils first. Now it's time to raid the freezer and cook all those items that you must either use or lose. The same basic rules apply as on Day One. Cook up as much of the good stuff as your family, friends, and neighbors can reasonably eat. Once the items have completely thawed, you should cook, give away, or chuck the rest.

Logic tells us to cook the most expensive stuff first, sacrificing the cheaper items, if necessary. (Keep in mind that, depending on the reason for the power outage and your insurance coverage, the loss of the contents of your fridge and freezer may be covered by your insurance policy—run a tab as you throw things out.) On subsequent days we made a good old-fashioned American BBQ (for us, veggie burgers and dogs) and a Mediterranean feast with hummus, couscous pilaf, and dolmas—made entirely with items from the pantry. Yum.

The day after Isabel, the skies were clear and blue, and virtually everyone with an outdoor grill was cooking outside. Whether your grill sizzles with veggie burgers, portobello mushroom caps, or meatier fare, this is the time when grilling out becomes more of a necessity than a whim, but it can be just as tasty. If at all possible, just for a time, try to immerse yourself in the fun of a cookout and forget the work and the waiting that still lie ahead.

Even during emergency cooking you will want to pay attention to basic nutritional guidelines. Whenever possible, be sure to include beans, nuts, or other protein and a variety of vegetables and fruit. Disasters sometimes dictate what you can eat, but if you have prepared your pantry well, you should still have lots of flexibility.

I Hear You're Single . . .

Most of the recipes in this book serve four modest portions. From experience I can tell you that two people with large appetites can probably polish off many of the recipes without help. But since leftovers are impractical, singles and couples may want to cut some of these recipes in half. If you do have leftovers, store them on ice or share with a friend or neighbor.

On to the Cooking

Let's huddle.

The next five chapters contain sixty-eight recipes that have been designed for simple and speedy preparation. They're so tasty your family will call you a genius. You just need to be familiar with the strange universe you are entering.

Why simple and why speedy? Because if the disaster aftermath stretches beyond your limits (more than a day), you will need to conserve your resources. It's about extending your resources as far as possible—remember 2004 when Florida was smashed and re-smashed by four hurricanes. Every time the lights came back on, another storm knocked them out again. You need clever cooking to get through something like that.

The preparation of these recipes has some things in common that you need to know about:

1. The recipes presume that you have used up most of your fresh and frozen foods and are now relying on your pantry items for cooking. Virtually all of the recipes can accommodate the inclusion of fresh vegetables as long as they can be cooked quickly (usually by slicing them thinly), so as not to waste fuel.

2. Since you will probably be using a single-burner stove, you can only

prepare one course at a time. Of course, salads, some desserts, and snacks, which require no heat, can go with the hot soups, stews, or entrées. Otherwise cook and eat the heated recipes in separate courses. It prolongs dinner, but what else do you have to do?

3. The recipes are designed to cook over a single-burner gas stove, often in ten minutes. You can sauté, you can boil, but, unless you have a working gas oven, you'll need to put off baking that trio of Mozart cakes for now.

4. Most of the recipes make four servings, but bear in mind that this means different things to different people, depending on whether you eat like sparrows or linebackers. If you and your clan have hearty appetites, you may find yourself looking for a second helping that doesn't exist. With that said, many of the recipes are easily doubled or, conversely, cut in half. If you prepare a recipe that doesn't stretch far enough for your hungry group, you can always prepare another recipe and turn the meal into your own version of a tasting menu. Better to prepare too little than too much.

5. Some of the recipes incorporate packaged instant products such as quick-cooking rice. Two of the recipes even use instant mashed potatoes. (There, I said it.)

6. The recipes are vegetarian. Not just because Robin and I are vegetarian but because you can't keep meat, fish, eggs, and dairy products

fresh without refrigeration. At your own discretion, however, you can add canned meat or seafood products to many of the recipes, either in place of beans or in addition to them. Other sources of meat or seafood are MREs, SREs, flash-frozen foods, or meals you previously dehydrated. Recipes using milk call for "milk or soy milk," allowing you to choose whichever you prefer. Both dairy milk and soy milk are available powdered or in shelf-stable aseptic containers (reconstitute only as much of powdered variety as you need, and after you open an aseptic container, be sure to finish it in one sitting as it will no longer keep unrefrigerated once opened). What the heck. It's not the worst thing in the world for Mother Nature to force you to go veg for a few days.

7. Good nutrition. These recipes and menu suggestions provide a broad spectrum of nutrients, vitamins, minerals, and protein. They will keep you healthy indefinitely.

With your temporary universe now defined, try to think "conservation" each time you cook. One way to do this is to observe the *mis en place* concept used in professional kitchens. The phrase literally means to "put in place" and involves setting up all the ingredients you will need to make the meal. Premeasure everything and place it conveniently near your burner before you turn on the gas.

> ### Boys and Grills
>
> Men generally run away from stoves, pans, and dishes. However, they draw near the barbecue grill just as Neanderthal huddled by the community fire. Grant them this attraction to grills gracefully and let them initiate the household boys into the timeless ritual. Why not? Family initiations in primitive societies galvanize a happy, safe household. Paint their faces. Give them marinade.

Now You're Cooking

By the third day without power, make sure you throw away any remaining refrigerated or frozen items. You'll be cooking from your pantry from now on.

The following chef's secrets will help you cook over open flames.

Most of the recipes in this book can be adapted for any heat source. If only a specific heat source is to be used, it will be specified in the particular recipe. It is vital that you conserve as much fuel as possible, so quick-cooking foods and those that simply need warming are your best bets. Après-disaster is not a good time to perfect your all-day bouillabaisse—you'll be out of cooking fuel before the pot begins to simmer. Besides, where will you get fresh fish, unless the hurricane blew some through your bay window? (This happened in the Charleston area during Hurricane Hugo—a half mile from the beach, one family found a dolphin in their living room.)

The recipes in this book were also designed to be adaptable to many different alternate cooking methods. So it's a good idea to have a contingency plan as well. While a few recipes use the last of the refrigerated items, the majority of the recipes in this book rely on pantry items. It's all one big cookout anyway.

When the power's off, we do most of our cooking on our indoor single-burner stove that uses a can of butane as fuel. We keep a case of extra fuel (a dozen cans) in the closet. That's enough fuel to keep us cooking for a few weeks. As a backup and for vari-

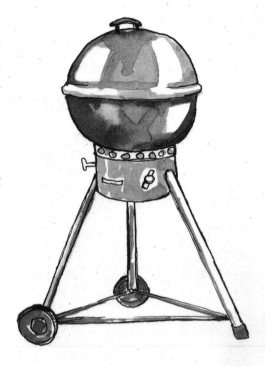

ety, we also have an outdoor gas grill, a wood-burning fireplace, a chafing dish, fondue pot, and Sterno. If we're without power long enough, we'd probably eventually use them all. But in general we've gotten by nicely using the butane cooker for most cooking and the outdoor grill for, well, grilling.

The Endless Cookout

Robin said my idea for grilled soup just won't fly, but here's another tip: Prepare the Ultimate Mixed Grill by slapping everything in the fridge and freezer onto the hot grill. Baste with marinade. Dinner is served. If you don't feel like cleaning the grill afterward, cut up veggies, douse with seasonings or a marinade or spice rub, and seal in portion-size envelopes of heavy-duty aluminum foil before grilling. Dub them "Foiled Again Dinner Packets" and amaze your family and friends.

Now that you have your equipment on hand and your pantry is bulging with food and other supplies, it's time to familiarize yourself with the recipes in this book. Sure, there'll be lots of time for reading once the power goes out, but still, you can never be too prepared, and you might actually want to have a dry run of cooking a meal without power, just for the practice. By this I don't mean go have a cookout or some other self-imposed al fresco dining. Try your hand at a real emergency meal—pretend you have no electricity whatsoever. Ignore your food processor and coffeemaker. See if you have what it takes to prepare recipes for disaster and dine in the dark. You may actually enjoy it.

Supplies You Can Count On

* aluminum foil for grilling
* disposable baby-bottle liners (when applicable)
* lamps and lamp oil
* manual can opener
* matches in a waterproof container
* medicine dropper
* needles and thread
* paper cups and plates and plastic utensils
* plastic sheeting
* plastic storage containers
* utility knife
* wrenches to turn off household gas and water

Advice for Best Use of this Book

You don't have to wait for a disaster to get your money's worth out of *Apocalypse Chow!* If you like to cook with jarred, freeze-dried, or canned goods, you won't find a cookbook anywhere that provides the same versatility, variety, and nutrition in meals that take less than fifteen minutes to prepare. Instructions for the recipes in the following chapters assume that you are using a gas grill, camp stove, or butane cooktop, but can also be adapted for cooking on wood fires and other heat sources. Have flame, will cook.

Grilling Tips

Make sure your grill is clean before using. Scrub it with a stiff brush, shunning soapy cleaners. Before heating, brush the clean grill with oil to prevent the food from sticking. To add an exotic flavor, try different types of wood such as cherry, hickory, or mesquite.

Chapter 5

Recipes for Disaster: Bean and Vegetable Main Dishes

Even if you secretly delight in an occasional can of beans, no one likes eating the same food every day. This chapter provides a variety of tasty main courses featuring the canned beans and vegetables from your Well-Tempered Pantry. When you want to transform cupboard stuff into gourmet meals, these are the recipes that can do it. They taste good and are packed with nutrients to give you and your fellow refugees ample protein, vitamins, and minerals. With your trusty butane burner you will transform your supply of pantry goods into luscious dishes such as Moroccan-Spiced Vegetable Stew, Polenta Fusion Fiesta, and Beat-the-Blahs Basic Black Bean Patties.

Bean and Vegetable Main Dishes

Garlicky Chickpeas with Potatoes and Tomatoes
Almost-Instant Black Bean Chili
Red Rum Chili
Moroccan-Spiced Vegetable Stew
Polenta Fusion Fiesta
"Great Personality" Hash
Beat-the-Blahs Basic Black Bean Patties
Curry in a Hurry
Wish-I-Were-in-Tuscany Chickpea Stew
Thaiphoon Stir-Fry
Rosemary-Scented Bricolage
High-Water Hoppin' John

Garlicky Chickpeas with Potatoes and Tomatoes

Canned chickpeas, also called garbanzos, combine with canned diced potatoes and tomatoes for a flavorful meal seasoned with garlic, herbs, and olive oil. For a complete one-dish meal add a drained can of chopped spinach or even cooked fresh greens if you're lucky enough to have some.

1   tablespoon olive oil

2   garlic cloves, minced

1   teaspoon dried basil

½ teaspoon dried savory

⅛ teaspoon or more red pepper flakes (optional)

One 16-ounce can diced white potatoes, drained

One 15.5-ounce can chickpeas, drained (and rinsed, if possible)

One 14.5-ounce can diced tomatoes, drained

Salt and freshly ground black pepper

1. Heat the oil in a large saucepan or skillet over medium heat. Add the garlic, basil, savory, and red pepper flakes, if using, and cook until fragrant, about 30 seconds.
2. Stir in the potatoes, chickpeas, and tomatoes, and then salt and pepper to taste. Cover and cook until the flavors are blended and the tomatoes are somewhat broken up and saucy, about 10 minutes.

Makes 4 servings

Almost-Instant Black Bean Chili

This hearty chili made with canned beans and a jar of salsa couldn't be easier. Cook it over any heat source, just long enough to heat through and marry the flavors. Serve over quick-cooking rice or noodles or eat it plain right out of the pot.

1. Combine the ingredients in a saucepan, reserving half the corn. Cover and cook over moderate heat, stirring occasionally. Add as much water as needed to create a sauce and to prevent mixture from sticking to the bottom of the pan.
2. Reduce heat to medium and simmer, stirring frequently until heated through, long enough to cook off any raw taste from the chili powder, about 15 minutes. Garnish with the remaining corn.

Makes 4 servings

Two 15.5-ounce cans black beans, drained (and rinsed, if possible)
One 16-ounce jar salsa (hot or mild)
2 to 3 tablespoons chili powder, or to taste
1 tablespoon dehydrated minced onion
One 8-ounce can corn, drained
1 cup water, or as needed

Red Rum Chili

Dark red kidney beans and a shot of dark rum. Yum. Yeah, this chili will put hair on your chest. With ground meat out of the question, add a cup of reconstituted TVP (textured vegetable protein) to make it heartier. Serve with crackers or corn bread, or ladle it over rice or noodles. Note: You can omit the rum, if you already used up your last drop in a batch of mai tais.

1 tablespoon olive oil

2 to 3 tablespoons chili powder

**One 15-ounce can
  crushed tomatoes**

**One 14.5-ounce can
  diced tomatoes, undrained**

**1 tablespoon dehydrated
  minced onion**

2 tablespoons dark rum

**One 4-ounce can chopped mild
  green chiles, drained**

**Two 15.5-ounce cans kidney beans,
  drained (and rinsed, if possible)**

**Salt and freshly ground black
  pepper**

1. Heat the oil in a large saucepan over medium heat. Stir in the chili powder, tomatoes, onion, and rum, stirring to blend.
2. Add the chiles, beans, and then salt and pepper to taste, and bring to a boil. Reduce heat to low and simmer, stirring occasionally until flavors are blended, about 15 minutes. Adjust seasonings to your tastes.

Makes 4 servings

Moroccan-Spiced Vegetable Stew

Fragrant spices and dried fruits lend a Moroccan flavor to this hearty stew that just begs to be served over couscous. (You can make your instant couscous first. Cover it to keep it warm until the stew is ready.)

1. Place the dried fruit and raisins or currants in a small heat-proof bowl. Add enough boiling water to cover your ingredients, and soak for 15 minutes to soften. Set aside.
2. In a large saucepan heat the oil over medium heat. Add the garlic, cumin, and cinnamon and cook, stirring for 30 seconds. Add the tomatoes, chickpeas, onion, and broth and bring to a boil.
3. Reduce heat to low, add the green beans, carrots, and reserved fruit. Season to taste with salt and pepper, and simmer, stirring occasionally until flavors are blended and desired consistency is reached, about 10 minutes.

Makes 4 servings

½ cup dried mixed fruit
¼ cup raisins or currants
1 tablespoon olive oil
1 garlic clove, minced
1 teaspoon ground cumin
1 teaspoon ground cinnamon
One 14.5-ounce can
diced tomatoes, drained
One 15.5-ounce can chickpeas,
drained (and rinsed, if possible)
1 tablespoon dehydrated
minced onion
1 ¼ cups vegetable broth
(see page 164)
One 15-ounce can green beans,
drained
One 8-ounce can sliced carrots,
drained
Salt and freshly ground
black pepper

Polenta Fusion Fiesta

Sure, polenta is Italian, but Homeland Security probably has better things to do than stop you from using your polenta with Mexican ingredients once in a while. Find your instant polenta in Italian food markets or gourmet specialty shops before disaster strikes. Not to be confused with those refrigerated tubes of polenta found in the produce section, look for precooked shelf-stable polenta on the grocer's shelf next to the pasta. An instant polenta mix is also available, in which case you'd prepare the polenta first, and then proceed with the recipe.

2 tablespoons olive oil

1 package precooked polenta,
 cut into ½-inch slices

One 14-ounce jar salsa
 (hot or mild)

One 15.5-ounce can pinto beans,
 drained (and rinsed, if possible)

One 8-ounce can corn, drained

One 4-ounce can chopped
 mild green chiles, drained

1 teaspoon dehydrated
 minced onion

½ teaspoon chili powder

Salt and freshly ground
 black pepper

1. Heat the olive oil in a skillet. Add the polenta slices and cook until brown on both sides. Set aside to keep warm.
2. In a saucepan, combine the remaining ingredients and heat until hot and the flavors are well blended. Spoon the salsa mixture over the polenta and serve.

Makes 4 servings

"Great Personality" Hash

Right. It's not much to look at, but it has great personality. This tasty dish is hard to stop eating once you start. Blot the ingredients before adding to the skillet and the hash will develop a crispy brown outer crust. Slather with ketchup, of course, but use Mrs. Dash or some other seasoning blend instead of salt to reign in the sodium a bit.

1. Heat the oil in large skillet over medium-high heat. Mash the potatoes a bit with a potato ricer till they are somewhat broken up, and add to the skillet along with the roasted red bell peppers, lentils, onion, and peas.
2. Drizzle with the tamari and season with the low-sodium seasoning blend and pepper to taste. Cook until hot and slightly browned, turning frequently with spatula, about 10 minutes.

Makes 4 servings

1 tablespoon olive oil
One 16-ounce can diced white potatoes, drained and blotted
One 7-ounce jar roasted red bell peppers, chopped and blotted
One 15.5-ounce can cooked lentils or kidney beans, drained and mashed
2 tablespoons dehydrated minced onion
One 8-ounce can green peas, drained, blotted, and mashed
1 tablespoon tamari or other soy sauce
Low-sodium seasoning blend such as Mrs. Dash, etc.
Freshly ground black pepper

Beat-the-Blahs Basic Black Bean Patties

These incredibly tasty patties can be served with a variety of sauces. It all depends on what flavor you're in the mood for. The spicy peanut sauce works great, but so do the salsa and the barbecue sauce.

One 16-ounce can diced white potatoes, drained
One 15.5-ounce can black beans, drained (and rinsed, if possible)
1 tablespoon dehydrated minced onion
1 teaspoon dried parsley
¾ cup dried bread crumbs
Salt and freshly ground black pepper
2 tablespoons olive oil

1. In a large bowl mash the potatoes and beans with a potato ricer until broken up. Add the onion, parsley, and bread crumbs, and then salt and pepper to taste. Mix until well combined.

2. Divide the mixture into six equal portions and use your hands to shape into patties.

3. Heat the oil in a large skillet over medium heat. Cook the bean patties until golden brown on both sides, about 5 minutes per side. Drain on paper towels and serve hot with your favorite sauce.

Makes 6 patties

Curry in a Hurry

No doubt about it, this curry is best served over rice. If you only have one available burner, make the rice first and cover and set aside until you make the curry. The rice will retain much of its heat. Because this curry goes together so quickly, the rice doesn't have a chance to cool down.

1. Heat the oil in a large saucepan over medium heat. Stir in the curry powder and cook until fragrant, about 30 seconds. Blend in the broth.
2. Add the kidney beans, green beans, potatoes, tomatoes, chiles, and onion, and bring to a boil.
3. Reduce the heat to low, and then season with salt and pepper to taste. Simmer for 10 minutes to blend the flavors. Serve over your premade rice.

Makes 4 servings

1 tablespoon canola oil

1 to 2 tablespoons curry powder, or to taste

1 ¼ cups vegetable broth (see page 164)

One 15.5-ounce can kidney beans, drained (and rinsed, if possible)

One 15-ounce can cut green beans, drained

One 16-ounce can diced white potatoes, drained

One 14.5-ounce can diced tomatoes, drained

One 4-ounce can chopped mild green chiles, drained

1 tablespoon dehydrated minced onion

Salt and freshly ground black pepper

Wish-I-Were-in-Tuscany Chickpea Stew

During an extended power outage you will wish that you were someplace else. As long as you're wishing, why not shoot for Tuscany? Pretend you're wolfing down this Tuscany-inspired stew in the courtyard of an Italian villa.

1 tablespoon olive oil

2 garlic cloves, minced

¼ cup dry white wine

½ teaspoon dried marjoram

Two 15.5-ounce cans chickpeas, drained (and rinsed, if possible)

One 15-ounce can diced white potatoes, drained

One 15-ounce can artichoke hearts, drained and chopped

One 6-ounce jar roasted red bell peppers, drained and chopped

1 tablespoon dehydrated minced onion

1 bay leaf

1 ¼ cups vegetable broth (see page 164)

Salt and freshly ground black pepper

1. Heat the oil in a large saucepan over medium heat. Add the garlic and cook until fragrant, about 30 seconds. Stir in the wine and marjoram.

2. Add the chickpeas, potatoes, artichoke hearts, bell peppers, onion, and bay leaf.

3. Stir in the broth and bring to a boil. Reduce the heat to low, season with salt and pepper to taste, and simmer to develop the flavors, about 10 minutes.

Makes 4 servings

Thaiphoon Stir-Fry

Culinary hardships abound during an emergency. During Hurricane Isabel we were unable to make our weekly pilgrimage to our favorite Thai restaurant. To comfort ourselves we whipped up this nifty stir-fry, using ingredients we had on hand.

1. Prepare the rice according to package directions. Cover and set aside.
2. Heat the oil in a large skillet over medium-high heat. Add ginger, garlic, tofu, red pepper flakes, and sugar, and stir-fry until the tofu is golden brown.
3. Add the soy sauce, mushrooms, Chinese vegetables, and chiles, and stir-fry until hot.
4. Serve over the rice and sprinkle with the peanuts.

Makes 4 servings

1 cup quick-cooking white or brown rice
1 tablespoon canola oil
2 teaspoons grated fresh ginger
1 garlic clove, minced
One 12-ounce box extra-firm tofu, well-drained, patted dry, and cut into 1-inch cubes
½ teaspoon red pepper flakes, or to taste
½ teaspoon sugar
2 tablespoons soy sauce
One 15-ounce can straw mushrooms, drained
One 15-ounce can Chinese vegetables, drained
One 4-ounce can chopped mild green chiles, drained
¼ cup dry-roasted peanuts

Rosemary-Scented Bricolage

Call it "stew made with odds and ends," and no one rushes to the table. But call it "bricolage," and you'll have them eating out of your hands. To use up fresh ingredients, make this stew within the first few days after the power goes out. When cooking hard root veggies, conserve fuel by cutting them as thin as possible, so they cook faster. If any of the ingredients is not on hand, leave it out and double up on what you do have, or substitute a different ingredient or a canned version of the fresh one. Almost anything goes: It's bricolage.

2 tablespoons olive oil

1 yellow onion, thinly sliced and chopped

2 garlic cloves, minced

2 potatoes, peeled and cut into ¼-inch cubes

2 carrots, peeled and thinly sliced

1 teaspoon fresh rosemary (or ½ teaspoon dried)

½ small head cabbage, finely shredded

One 15.5-ounce can white beans, drained (and rinsed, if possible)

1 ½ cups vegetable broth (see page 164)

Salt and freshly ground black pepper

1. Heat the oil in a large saucepan over medium heat. Add the onion, garlic, potatoes, carrots, and rosemary. Cover and cook, stirring occasionally until vegetables soften, about 5 minutes.
2. Add the cabbage, beans, broth, and then salt and pepper to taste, and bring to a boil. Reduce heat, cover, and simmer until vegetables are tender, about 15 minutes. Adjust seasonings.

Makes 4 servings

High-Water Hoppin' John

Southerners eat Hoppin' John and collards on New Year's Day for prosperity and good fortune in the coming year. Come hell or high water you can make an emergency variation of this good-luck dish. Usually fresh collard greens are cooked separately and served as a side, but in this version the canned greens are stirred in for a tasty one-dish meal. A liberal dose of Tabasco can be added at table by those who enjoy it.

1. Prepare the rice according to package directions. Add the onion, olive oil, and thyme. Reduce heat to low.
2. Stir in the black-eyed peas, collards, and then salt and pepper to taste. Heat until hot, about 5 minutes.
3. Serve with Tabasco at the table.

Makes 4 servings

1 cup quick-cooking white or brown rice
1 tablespoon dehydrated onion
1 tablespoon olive oil
½ teaspoon dried thyme
One 15.5-ounce can black-eyed peas, drained (and rinsed, if possible)
One 15-ounce can collard greens, drained
Salt and freshly ground black pepper
Tabasco

Rinse If Possible?

Some recipes ask that you rinse canned beans and other ingredients "if possible." Normally, canned beans are drained in a colander, and then rinsed under cold water, but if your taps are dry, you won't want to waste potable water rinsing beans. Don't worry about it—the beans will still be fine to eat.

Can Size

Recipes often call for specific can sizes, but you don't have to be a stickler. If the recipe calls for a 15.5-ounce can, and all you can find is a 16-ouncer, go with it—use what's available. That goes for smaller can sizes too.

Faux Meats

If you've never tried them before, you'll be surprised by how good faux, or "mock," meats can be. When the power is off, frozen products won't do you much good, but Worthington foods and other companies make a variety of canned vegetarian meats. These goodies work very well on skewers or in stews. Since they are precooked, you only need to heat them up for a few minutes. For a complete list of heat-and-serve vegetarian meats visit www.healthy-eating.com.

Chapter 6

Cooking Up a Storm: Pasta and Grain Main Dishes

These main-dish recipes use pasta and grains in creative and resourceful ways. Not only that, they require a minimum of preparation and cooking time in order to conserve precious fuel. They boast good nutrition and look and taste terrific. You're not eating mere survival grub here—no way—these dishes teeter perilously close to haute cuisine.

Think of it: No power, and you're making recipes such as Orecchiette with White Beans and Olivada and Rice Noodles with Spicy Peanut Sauce, as long as you have a heat source that can bring water to a boil. These dishes taste so good, you may want to make them even when the power is on.

You will notice that some of the recipes call for ultrathin pasta strands such as capellini. This is because they cook up in less than five minutes. When power is at a premium and pasta is on the menu, "thin is in" to save your precious fuel.

Pasta and Grain Main Dishes

Kitchen Sink Capellini

Pasta Improv

Puttanesca in a Pinch

Orecchiette with White Beans and Olivada

Last-Resort Lasagne

"Duck and Cover" Tortilla Bake

Rice Noodles with Spicy Peanut Sauce

High-Road Lo Mein

Jazzed-Up Jasmine Rice

Best-of-It Bulgur Pilaf

Quick Quinoa Pilaf

Going-with-the-Grain Red Beans and Rice

Consolation Couscous

Suddenly Sushi

Kitchen Sink Capellini

While others in your neighborhood may be eating canned SpaghettiOs, you can feast on this elegant dish made with fodder from your pantry. Regular black olives are used because they're available in small cans, but if you're fortunate enough to have some kalamata or other good olives on hand, use them instead. Since this has so many goodies in it, you can leave one or two items out if you want to, and it will still taste great.

1. Place the sun-dried tomatoes in a small heat-proof bowl. Add boiling water and let sit for 10 minutes to soften. Drain and cut into 1/4-inch strips. Set aside.
2. Cook the pasta in a large pot of boiling salted water until just tender, about 4 minutes.
3. Drain the pasta in a colander. Drizzle with 1 tablespoon of the olive oil, toss to coat, and set aside.
4. In the same pot, heat the remaining oil over medium heat. Add the garlic and cook until fragrant, about 30 seconds. Stir in both kinds of tomatoes, chickpeas, artichoke hearts, olives, capers (if using), basil, and then salt and pepper to taste. Cook over medium heat until hot, about 5 minutes.
5. Add the reserved pasta and toss gently to combine and heat through. Sprinkle with the pine nuts, if desired, and serve immediately.

½ cup sun-dried tomatoes
1 pound capellini
2 tablespoons olive oil
2 garlic cloves, finely minced
One 28-ounce can diced tomatoes, drained
One 8-ounce can chickpeas, drained (and rinsed, if possible)
One 6-ounce jar marinated artichoke hearts, drained and chopped
One 4-ounce can sliced black olives, drained
1 tablespoon capers, drained (optional)
1 teaspoon dried basil (or 1 tablespoon fresh basil, if available)
Salt and freshly ground black pepper
¼ cup toasted pine nuts (optional)

Makes 4 servings

Pasta Improv

Sure, a jarred pasta sauce is easier, but if you feel like improvising your own tomato sauce, here's an easy way to do it. This flavorful sauce is made with pantry ingredients. However, fresh ingredients, such as an onion, tomatoes, or fresh herbs, may be used if you have them on hand. Be sure to use fresh garlic if you can, since garlic bulbs are fine at room temperature. If you don't have fresh, substitute a small amount of garlic powder.

1 pound pasta of choice
2 tablespoons olive oil
2 garlic cloves, chopped
One 28-ounce can
   crushed tomatoes
1 tablespoon dehydrated
   minced onion
2 tablespoons dry
   red wine
¼ teaspoon red pepper
   flakes
1 tablespoon dried basil
1 teaspoon dried parsley
Salt and freshly ground
   black pepper

1. Cook the pasta in a pot of boiling salted water according to package directions. Drain well, toss with 1 tablespoon of the olive oil, and set aside while you make the sauce.
2. Heat the remaining oil in the same pot over medium heat. Add the garlic and cook until fragrant, about 30 seconds. Stir in the tomatoes, onion, wine, red pepper flakes, basil, and parsley. Season to taste with salt and pepper, and simmer until hot.
3. Stir in the cooked pasta until heated through, tossing gently to combine.

Makes 4 servings

Puttanesca in a Pinch

The name of this piquant pasta sauce means "streetwalker style," supposedly because ladies of the evening prepare it at the end of a long night's work. Imported black and green olives are best in this sauce, but if all you have is the regular supermarket variety, they can be used in a pinch.

1. Cook the pasta in a large pot of boiling salted water, stirring occasionally, until it is al dente. Drain the pasta and place in a large bowl, tossing with a little olive oil to prevent sticking.
2. Heat the remaining oil in the same pot over medium heat. Add the garlic and cook until fragrant, about 30 seconds. Stir in the tomatoes, black and green olives, capers, red pepper flakes, and parsley. Season with salt and pepper to taste. Reduce heat to low and simmer for 10 minutes to blend flavors, stirring occasionally.
3. Add the reserved pasta and toss gently to combine and heat through.

Makes 4 servings

1 pound pasta of choice
2 tablespoons olive oil
3 large garlic cloves, finely chopped
One 28-ounce can crushed tomatoes
½ cup pitted and sliced imported black olives (or one 4-ounce can sliced black olives, drained)
¼ cup pitted and sliced green olives
2 tablespoons capers, drained and chopped
½ teaspoon red pepper flakes
1 teaspoon dried parsley
Salt and freshly ground black pepper

Orecchiette with White Beans and Olivada

If you're lucky enough to have imported olives on hand, make olivada, a rich Mediterranean olive paste that goes great with pasta. (Add capers, and you have tapenade.) It's best to use a mortar and pestle to mash these babies, but you can finely chop the olives and garlic with a knife or run them through a food grinder as well. Be advised: This recipe is for card-carrying olive lovers. Although they take longer to cook than thin strands, we're partial to orecchiette ("little ears") in this recipe. Use whatever you've got.

8 ounces gaeta or other imported black olives, pitted

1 large garlic clove

2 teaspoons freshly squeezed lemon juice

½ teaspoon dried basil

Salt and freshly ground black pepper

¼ cup olive oil

1 pound orecchiette pasta

One 15.5-ounce can Great Northern or other white beans, drained (and rinsed, if possible)

1. Finely chop the olives and garlic. Transfer to a mortar and pestle and add the lemon juice, basil, and then salt and pepper to taste. Work the mixture until blended. Slowly add the olive oil and blend to a paste. Set aside.

2. Cook the orecchiette in a large pot of boiling salted water, stirring occasionally, until it is al dente, about 8 to 10 minutes. Remove 1 to 2 tablespoons of the hot pasta water and blend it into the olivada.

3. Place the beans in the colander and drain the pasta over the beans. This will heat and rinse the beans at the same time. Place the drained pasta and beans in a large serving bowl. Add the olivada and toss gently to combine. Serve hot.

Makes 4 servings

Last-Resort Lasagne

This is as close as you're going to get to real lasagne in a voltless kitchen, but the results are surprisingly good. The key to success is the no-bake lasagna noodles. You can jazz this up by adding TVP granules or a can of drained sliced mushrooms to the tomato sauce. You can make homemade tomato sauce if you prefer, but the prepared sauce works great and will save fuel (and pot-washing).

1. In a bowl combine the beans, tofu, 2 tablespoons of the cheese, parsley, basil, oregano, onion, and then salt and pepper to taste. Mash with a potato ricer until smooth and well combined. Taste to adjust seasoning.
2. In a large skillet over medium-low heat, spread one cup of the sauce at the bottom of the skillet. Arrange 3 lasagna noodles on top of sauce, overlapping slightly.
3. Spread half of the tofu and bean mixture on top of the lasagna, and then top with 3 more noodles. Spread a small amount of sauce on top and spread the remaining filling mixture over it.
4. Top with the remaining 3 lasagna noodles and cover with the last of the sauce. Sprinkle the remaining cheese (or as much as you like) to cover the sauce.
5. Cover skillet tightly with a lid and cook until the noodles are tender and the filling is hot, about 15 minutes.
6. Remove from heat and let stand for 5 minutes before serving.

One 15.5-ounce can white beans, drained (and rinsed, if possible)
One 12-ounce box firm silken tofu, drained
1 small container grated regular or soy Parmesan cheese
1 teaspoon dried parsley
¼ teaspoon dried basil
¼ teaspoon dried oregano
¼ teaspoon dehydrated minced onion
Salt and freshly ground black pepper
One 28-ounce jar tomato-based pasta sauce of choice
9 sheets no-bake lasagna noodles

Makes 4 servings

"Duck and Cover" Tortilla Bake

Salsa, chiles, pinto beans, and tortillas team up for a zesty "baked" casserole. If you have any regular or soy cheddar cheese available, shred it on top. Otherwise a light dusting of Parmesan cheese from one of those shaker containers works to good effect.

One 15.5-ounce can pinto beans, drained (and rinsed, if possible)
One 4-ounce can chopped mild green chiles, drained
½ teaspoon chili powder, or more to taste
¼ teaspoon dried oregano
One 16-ounce jar salsa (hot or mild)
Salt and freshly ground black pepper
Eight 8-inch flour tortillas
Grated regular or soy Parmesan or other cheese (optional)

1. In a bowl, combine the pinto beans, chiles, chili powder, and oregano. Stir in half the salsa and mix well. Season with salt and pepper to taste. Mash the pinto mixture with a potato ricer to break up ingredients. Set aside.
2. Cover the bottom of a deep skillet with half of the remaining salsa. Top with half of the tortillas, overlapping as necessary. Cover the tortillas with the reserved pinto mixture, then layer with the remaining tortillas. Spread the remaining salsa over all.
3. Cover with a tight-fitting lid and cook over a low flame for 15 minutes to heat through. Sprinkle with Parmesan or other cheese, if available.

Makes 4 servings

Rice Noodles with Spicy Peanut Sauce

If you don't have rice noodles, you can use any regular pasta instead. Simply cook according to package directions and add to the sauce. Our local supermarket carries canned stir-fry vegetables—a combination of water chestnuts, bamboo shoots, bean sprouts, and baby corn. If unavailable, use a small can of your choice of two of those ingredients, or others you may prefer, such as straw mushrooms.

1. Soak the noodles in boiling water until soft, about 15 minutes. While the noodles are softening, prepare the sauce.
2. In a bowl, whisk together the peanut butter, tamari, lime juice, sugar, red pepper flakes, and 1/2 cup of the water. Blend until smooth.
3. Transfer the peanut sauce to a large pot and stir in as much of the remaining water as needed to give it a desirable consistency. Heat the sauce over low heat, stirring occasionally. Add the vegetables and heat through until hot. Keep warm.
4. Drain the softened noodles and add to the pot. Toss gently to combine with the peanut sauce. Serve sprinkled with peanuts.

Makes 4 servings

8 ounces flat rice noodles
½ cup peanut butter
3 tablespoons tamari or other soy sauce
2 teaspoons fresh lime juice
1 teaspoon brown sugar
½ teaspoon red pepper flakes
1 cup water
One 15-ounce can stir-fry vegetables, drained
2 tablespoons chopped roasted peanuts

High-Road Lo Mein

With no fresh veggies in sight, you can take the high road and make lo mein with what you have. To save water, rinse the water chestnuts and bamboo shoots when you pour out the water after cooking the noodles. This is a good recipe to add on. That is, if you make this when you still have frozen veggies to use up, add some thawed frozen green peas or snow peas for color. A shredded fresh carrot is great too, if you have one. Spice it up with a drizzle of Chinese hot oil.

One 8-ounce can water chestnuts, drained

One 8-ounce can bamboo shoots, drained

12 ounces Chinese noodles or linguine

2 teaspoons toasted sesame oil

¼ cup tamari or other soy sauce

3 tablespoons dry sherry

Pinch of sugar

1 tablespoon canola oil

2 shallots, halved lengthwise and thinly sliced

2 teaspoons grated fresh ginger

1 carrot (if you have one), shredded

1. Drain the water chestnuts and bamboo shoots in the colander and set aside while you prepare the noodles.
2. Cook the noodles in a pot of boiling water until tender. Drain well into the colander containing the drained water chestnuts and bamboo shoots. Add 1 teaspoon of the sesame oil, tossing to coat. Set aside.
3. To make the sauce, in a small bowl combine the tamari, sherry, sugar, and remaining sesame oil. Set aside.
4. Heat the canola oil in the same pot over medium heat. Add the shallots, ginger, and carrot (if using) and stir-fry for 1 minute. Add the reserved noodles, water chestnuts, bamboo shoots, and the sauce, and stir-fry to combine and heat through until hot, about 3 minutes.

Makes 4 servings

Jazzed-Up Jasmine Rice

You'll need to cook the rice first, and then let it cool down a bit before making this recipe. If canned stir-fry vegetables are unavailable, substitute a can of mixed vegetables or fine slivers of any fresh veggies you may have on hand, such as carrots or onions.

1. Heat the oil in a large skillet over medium-high heat. Add the ginger and cook until fragrant, about 30 seconds.
2. Add the vegetables and rice, and stir-fry until combined. Add the soy sauce and sugar, and stir-fry until the ingredients are blended and hot, about 5 minutes.
3. Sprinkle with chopped cashews and serve hot.

Makes 4 servings

1 tablespoon canola oil
1 tablespoon grated fresh ginger
One 15-ounce can mixed vegetables, drained
3 ½ cups cooked jasmine rice
2 tablespoons tamari
½ teaspoon light brown sugar
½ cup chopped roasted cashew nuts

Best-of-It Bulgur Pilaf

Also called cracked wheat, bulgur is a quick-cooking grain with a hearty nutlike flavor that is used to make the popular Middle Eastern salad, tabbouleh. When being electricity-challenged gets you down, this yummy pilaf with sweet-tart cranberries and crunchy almonds will help you make the best of it.

2 cups vegetable broth (see page 164)
1 cup medium bulgur
1 tablespoon dehydrated minced onion
Salt and freshly ground black pepper
½ cup dried cranberries
½ cup toasted slivered almonds
1 teaspoon dried parsley or mint (or 1 tablespoon fresh, if you've got it)

1. Bring the broth to a boil in a large saucepan. Add the bulgur and onion and stir to combine. Reduce the heat to low and season with salt and pepper to taste. Cover and simmer until the bulgur is tender and the liquid is absorbed, about 8 minutes.
2. Remove the pan from the heat and stir in the cranberries, almonds, and parsley or mint. Cover and let stand for 10 minutes before serving.

Makes 4 servings

Quick Quinoa Pilaf

Extremely high in protein and quick-cooking to boot, quinoa is an ideal grain for emergency meals. It adapts deliciously to various seasoning palettes and is especially delicious when prepared pilaf-style. Quinoa is available in natural food stores. (Did you know it was eaten by the Incas?)

1. Rinse the quinoa well to remove the bitter white coating. Drain it thoroughly and set aside.
2. Bring the broth or water to a boil. Add the quinoa and onion. Reduce the heat to low and season to taste with salt and pepper. Cover and cook until the water is absorbed, about 12 minutes.
3. Remove from heat, stir in the carrots, peas, pine nuts, and chives. Serve hot.

Makes 4 servings

1 ½ cups quinoa
3 cups vegetable broth
(see page 164) or water
1 tablespoon dehydrated
minced onion
Salt and freshly ground
black pepper
One 8-ounce can sliced carrots,
drained
One 8-ounce can green peas,
drained
¼ cup toasted pine nuts
1 tablespoon dried chives

Going-with-the-Grain Red Beans and Rice

Brown rice is more nutritious than white and is available in a quick-cooking version that takes only ten minutes to cook. Quick-cooking white rice may be used if you prefer.

1 tablespoon olive oil

2 garlic cloves, minced

2 cups quick-cooking brown or white rice

1 tablespoon dehydrated minced onion

One 4-ounce can chopped mild green chiles, drained

½ teaspoon salt

¼ teaspoon dried thyme

Pinch of ground nutmeg

2 ¼ cups water

One 15.5-ounce can kidney beans, drained (and rinsed, if possible)

1. Heat the oil in a saucepan over medium heat. Add the garlic and cook until fragrant, about 30 seconds. Stir in the rice to coat with oil. Add the onion, chiles, salt, thyme, and nutmeg, stirring to combine.
2. Stir in the water, cover, and cook until the rice is tender, 8 to 10 minutes. Stir in the beans and cook until hot, about 5 minutes longer. Adjust seasonings to your tastes.

Makes 4 servings

Consolation Couscous

What do you do when you're famished and don't feel like slaving over a hot butane stove? Console yourself with this almost-instant couscous pilaf. It's tasty, filling, and ready in ten minutes. If you have a fresh carrot, you can substitute it for the canned vegetables. Simply shred the carrot on a box grater and add it when you add the couscous. The bits of carrot will soften up nicely.

1. Bring the water to a boil in a saucepan. Stir in the couscous and the onion. Cover, turn off the heat, and let the mixture sit for 10 minutes.
2. Stir in the chickpeas, vegetables, pecans, and raisins. Season to taste with salt and pepper, and serve.

Makes 4 servings

2 cups water or vegetable broth (see page 164)
1 cup couscous
1 tablespoon dehydrated minced onion
One 15.5-ounce can chickpeas, drained (and rinsed, if possible)
One 15-ounce can mixed vegetables, drained
½ cup chopped pecans or slivered almonds
¼ cup golden or regular raisins
Salt and freshly ground black pepper

Suddenly Sushi

Once you cook the rice, the rest is playtime. Sushi-making ingredients are available at well-stocked supermarkets, natural-food stores, and Asian markets. Note: To save fuel this sushi is made with quick-cooking rice instead of traditional sushi rice, which is glutinous and holds together better. Since quick-cooking rice is a bit looser, you'll need to press the rice into the nori a bit more, so it holds together. Of course, if fuel is not a problem, consider making real sushi rice instead.

2 cups quick-cooking white rice
2 tablespoons rice vinegar
1 tablespoon sugar
½ teaspoon salt
6 roasted nori sheets
2 tablespoons toasted
   sesame seeds
Filling ingredients (see box)
1 tablespoon wasabi powder
1 tablespoon warm water
2 tablespoons pickled ginger
  (for garnish)
Tamari

Filling suggestions (choose two):
canned asparagus spears, drained and patted dry; hearts of palm, cut into strips; kanpyo, reconstituted; roasted red peppers, cut into strips; fried wheat gluten, cut into strips

1. Cook the rice in boiling water according to package directions. Transfer the rice to a shallow bowl and mix in the vinegar, sugar, and salt. Spread the rice evenly using a rice paddle or large wooden spoon. Set aside to cool.
2. Place a sheet of nori on a sudare (bamboo sushi mat) or a cloth napkin. Spread ½ cup of the rice evenly over the nori sheet—to the edge on the sides and to within 1 inch on the top and bottom edges. Sprinkle the rice evenly with the sesame seeds. Along the edge nearest to you, place a row of filling ingredients on top of the rice.
3. Beginning at the side nearest you, roll up the sudare, pressing firmly against the nori to roll around the ingredients, using your fingers to keep the end of the sudare from rolling into the sushi. Continue rolling slowly up to the top edge. Wet the exposed edge of the nori with a bit of water to seal the roll. Gently squeeze the sudare around the sushi roll and remove the mat.
4. Use a sharp knife to cut the sushi roll into 6 pieces, wiping the blade between cuts. Stand the pieces on end and place on a large platter. Make additional rolls with the remaining ingredients.
5. In a small bowl combine the wasabi powder with the warm water to form a paste. Place a small mound of the wasabi paste onto the sushi platter. Arrange a pile of pickled ginger on the platter as well. Pour tamari into small dipping bowls to serve alongside the rolls.

Makes 6 rolls or 36 sushi pieces

The Vast Pasta Universe

Capellini, or angel hair, and other thin pastas such as vermicelli will be your best bet when power goes out, since they cook in less than five minutes, thus saving precious fuel. Spaghetti and several other pastas only take eight to ten minutes, so don't discount them. Keep a good supply of cooking fuel on hand, so you can enjoy a wide range of pasta and grains.

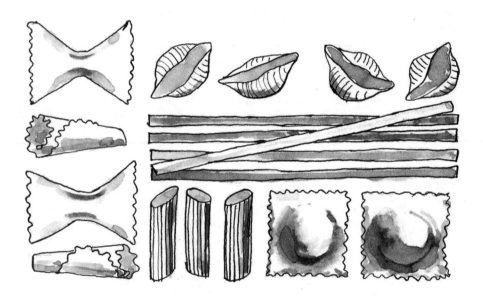

Vegetable Grilling for the Common Man

Grilling vegetables over a flame caramelizes their natural sugars and intensifies the flavors, so go ahead and grill any remaining fresh produce such as bell peppers, eggplant, portobello mushrooms, and fennel bulbs. Cut them into uniform pieces; brush with olive oil, a marinade, or spice rub; and place on the grill. The vegetables can also be threaded onto wooden or metal skewers and served over pasta or rice.

Grain Cooking

Although many grains can take up to forty-five minutes to cook, there are others that barely need cooking at all. Couscous is a prime example, taking just five minutes to cook. Be sure to stock up on the whole-grain variety for optimum nutrition. Other quick-cooking grains include bulgur, the steamed and crushed wheat kernels used to make tabbouleh, and kasha, also known as buckwheat groats, popular in eastern European countries.

Chapter 7

Dining in the Dark: Salad Days

During long monotonous days with no power, you will appreciate having variety.

"But there's no lettuce," you complain indignantly. "The fresh produce spoiled days ago."

Well, you may be as surprised as I was that you don't have to have big green leaves to make a salad. And it isn't a lot of work, either. This delicious dozen will add color, texture, and extra flavor with the vegetables waiting for you in your emergency larder. Many of the salads make use of quick-cooking grains and noodles along with beans and nuts to make them substantial enough to serve as a main dish for lunch or a light supper.

It's important to note that many of these salads would be even better if served on a bed of salad greens (if it's early in the game and you still have some, or if they're growing in your garden), so serve 'em if you've got 'em.

Salad Days

Calm-Down Couscous Salad

"Make Mine Moroccan" Couscous Salad

Tournedos of Tabbouleh Salad

Pantry Pasta Salad with Artichokes, Chickpeas, and Sun-Dried Tomatoes

Composed Marinated Vegetable Salad

Corn, Tomatillo, and Red Pepper Salad

Nutty Ramen Salad

Southwest Salmagundi

"Three's a Crowd" Bean Salad

"We're Not in Provence Anymore" *Salade Nicoise*

Crunchy Asian Salad with Peanut Dressing

Hearts of Palm Salad with Limas, Black Olives,

and Roasted Red Pepper Strips

Calm-Down Couscous Salad

Couscous is ideal for emergency cooking since it doesn't take long to cook. Be sure to stock up on the whole-grain variety for optimum nutrition. As is, the recipe is a main-dish salad for four but can be easily halved for two.

2 ½ cups water
One cube of vegetable bouillon
2 cups whole-grain couscous
½ cup slivered almonds, lightly toasted
2 teaspoons dried parsley flakes (or 2 tablespoons fresh parsley, if available)
3 tablespoons olive oil
1 ½ tablespoons white wine vinegar
2 teaspoons dried minced chives
Salt and freshly ground pepper
Two 16-ounce jars three-bean salad, drained

1. In a saucepan combine the water and bouillon cube and bring to a boil. Stir in the couscous, cover the saucepan, and remove it from the heat. Let the mixture stand for 5 minutes.
2. Stir in the almonds, parsley, olive oil, vinegar, chives, and then salt and pepper to taste. Mix well.
3. Mound in the center of a platter surrounded by three-bean salad.

Makes 4 servings

"Make Mine Moroccan" Couscous Salad

Exotic spices make this salad the one to choose when you want something that will slap you awake. It takes only a few minutes to prepare.

1. Heat 1/2 tablespoon of the oil in a medium saucepan over low heat. Add the turmeric, ginger, cinnamon, cumin, cayenne, and couscous and stir until fragrant, about 1 minute. Do not burn. Stir in the water and juice and bring to a boil. Reduce the heat to very low, cover, and cook 5 minutes. Remove from heat and let stand about 5 minutes longer.
2. Transfer the couscous to a large bowl, using a fork to fluff it up. Stir in the remaining 1/2 tablespoon of oil, sugar, and salt to taste.
3. Add the chickpeas, carrots, dried fruit, and raisins. Toss gently to combine. Garnish with peanuts.

Makes 4 servings

1 tablespoon olive oil
¼ teaspoon ground turmeric
¼ teaspoon ground ginger
¼ teaspoon ground cinnamon
¼ teaspoon ground cumin
¼ teaspoon cayenne pepper
1 ½ cups couscous
1 ¼ cups water
1 cup apple juice
1 teaspoon light brown sugar
  or a natural sweetener
Salt
One 15.5-ounce can chickpeas,
  drained (and rinsed, if possible)
One 8-ounce can sliced carrots,
  drained
¼ cup chopped dried fruit
¼ cup golden raisins
2 tablespoons chopped
  unsalted peanuts

Tournedos of Tabbouleh Salad

You can merely spoon this salad onto a plate or play with your food. Form your tabbouleh into fun shapes: a Mayan pyramid, Mt. Rushmore, or something more naughty. Or how about little mounds shaped like tournedos of beef? Use ring molds, if you have them, or cut the bottom off an empty, squat 4-ounce can, such as one containing green chiles.

2 cups water

1 cup bulgur

1 tablespoon dehydrated onion

One 14.5-ounce can diced tomatoes, drained and chopped

One 15.5-ounce can chickpeas, drained (and rinsed, if possible)

1 teaspoon dried parsley (or 1 tablespoon fresh, if available)

½ teaspoon dried mint (or 1 teaspoon fresh, if available)

⅓ cup olive oil

2 tablespoons fresh lemon juice

Salt and freshly ground black pepper

1. Bring the water to a boil and add the bulgur and onion. Reduce heat to low, cover, and simmer for 15 minutes, or until water is absorbed. Drain any remaining water and blot the bulgur to remove excess moisture.
2. Place the bulgur in a bowl and allow it to cool. Add the tomatoes, chickpeas, parsley, and mint.
3. To make the dressing, in a small bowl combine the olive oil, lemon juice, and then salt and pepper to taste. Pour the dressing over the salad and toss well to combine.
4. To serve, place a ring mold on a salad plate and pack the salad mixture inside. Remove mold and repeat, making two tournedos per serving.

Makes 4 servings

Pantry Pasta Salad with Artichokes, Chickpeas, and Sun-Dried Tomatoes

The great thing about this recipe is that the portion size is easy to adjust. This version makes four average servings, or enough for two or three hungry eaters. To increase the volume, cook up an entire pound of pasta and add additional pantry goodies, either more of the same or new ones such as olives, roasted red peppers, or pine nuts.

1. Cook the pasta in a pot of boiling salted water, stirring occasionally, until al dente, 8 to 10 minutes.
2. Drain the chickpeas into a colander and, when the pasta is cooked, drain it into the same strainer, allowing the pasta water to rinse the chickpeas. Transfer the pasta and chickpeas to a large bowl, toss with 1 teaspoon of the olive oil, and set aside.
3. In a small bowl combine the lemon juice, tarragon, and then salt and pepper to taste. Whisk in the remaining olive oil until blended, and pour dressing over pasta. Add the artichokes and sun-dried tomatoes, and toss to combine.

Makes 4 servings

12 ounces rotini or other pasta shape
One 15.5-ounce can chickpeas, drained (and rinsed, if possible)
¼ cup plus 1 teaspoon olive oil
2 tablespoons lemon juice
1 teaspoon dried tarragon
Salt and freshly ground black pepper
One 6-ounce can marinated artichoke hearts, drained
3 to 4 sun-dried tomatoes, reconstituted and cut into thin strips

Composed Marinated Vegetable Salad

Despite its humble origins in your pantry hoard, this salad draws its inspiration from both a French *salade composée* and an Italian antipasto, wherein you artfully arrange the salad components on a platter.

¼ cup olive oil

2 tablespoons balsamic vinegar

½ teaspoon minced garlic

½ teaspoon dried basil

Salt and freshly ground black pepper

One 8-ounce can cut green beans, drained

One 4-ounce jar roasted red bell peppers, drained and cut into strips

One 8-ounce can sliced potatoes, drained

One 4-ounce jar marinated artichoke hearts, drained

One 3-ounce can ripe, pitted black olives, drained

2 tablespoons toasted pine nuts

1. To make the dressing, in a small bowl combine the olive oil, balsamic vinegar, garlic, basil, salt, and pepper. Whisk to blend. Set aside.
2. Arrange the green beans, bell peppers, potatoes, and artichoke hearts on a large platter. Drizzle the dressing evenly and nestle the olives decoratively among the vegetables. Sprinkle with pine nuts and serve.

Makes 4 servings

Corn, Tomatillo, and Red Pepper Salad

To turn this into a main-dish salad, just add a can of pinto beans. It will add extra protein without disrespecting the Southwestern theme.

1. In a large bowl combine the corn, tomatillos, and bell peppers.
2. To make the dressing, in a small bowl combine the shallot, lime juice, cumin, salt, and cayenne. Whisk in the oil to emulsify.
3. Pour the dressing over the salad and toss lightly to coat. Adjust seasonings to your tastes.

Makes 4 servings

One 15-ounce can corn, drained
One 14-ounce can tomatillos, drained and chopped
One 8-ounce can roasted red bell peppers, drained and chopped
1 shallot, minced
2 tablespoons lime juice
¼ teaspoon ground cumin
½ teaspoon salt
⅛ teaspoon cayenne pepper
¼ cup olive oil

Nutty Ramen Salad

After slurping your umpteenth bowl of instant ramen noodle soup, you may be looking for a different way to prepare that intrepid noodle brick. How about turning it into a salad? Sounds nutty, but tastes delicious (and nutty too, thanks to the slivered almonds).

**2 packages ramen noodles,
  broken up into 1-inch pieces**
1 tablespoon dehydrated onion
One 14-ounce can bean sprouts
¼ cup toasted sesame oil
1 cup slivered almonds
¼ cup sunflower seeds
¼ cup sesame seeds
6 tablespoons rice wine vinegar
1 tablespoon sugar
**2 seasoning packets from
  ramen noodles**
**1 tablespoon tamari or other
  soy sauce**

1. Place the noodles and onion in a small saucepan of boiling water. Reduce heat to low, cook for 1 minute. Drain the bean sprouts in a colander, and when the noodles are cooked, drain them in the same strainer to rinse the bean sprouts. Transfer the noodles and bean sprouts to a bowl and set aside.

2. Heat 2 tablespoons toasted sesame oil in a skillet over medium heat. Add the almonds and cook, stirring until golden brown, about 5 minutes. Add the sunflower and sesame seeds and continue to cook until sesame seeds turn golden brown, 1 to 2 minutes longer. Add to the noodle mixture and toss to combine.

3. Add the vinegar, remaining sesame oil, sugar, ramen seasoning, and tamari, stirring constantly to dissolve and coat the ingredients. Cover and let stand for 15 minutes before serving.

Makes 4 servings

Southwest Salmagundi

Spicy-food lovers may want to use hot salsa rather than mild. The asbestos-tongued may go a step further and substitute a small can of sliced jalapeños for the mild green chiles.

1. In a large bowl combine the pinto beans, chiles, parsley, olive oil, lime juice, cumin, chili powder, garlic powder, and salt to taste. Stir gently to combine.
2. Spread the heated refried beans in the center of a large plate, mound the pinto bean salad on top, and arrange a border of salsa around the outside perimeter of the salad. Surround with tortilla chips.

Makes 4 servings

One 15.5-ounce can pinto beans, drained (and rinsed, if possible)
One 4-ounce can chopped mild green chiles, drained
1 teaspoon dried parsley
3 tablespoons olive oil
1 tablespoon lime juice
¼ teaspoon ground cumin
¼ teaspoon chili powder
⅛ teaspoon garlic powder
Salt
One 16-ounce can refried beans beans, heated
One 8-ounce jar salsa (hot or mild)
Tortilla chips, as desired

"Three's a Crowd" Bean Salad

If you find you've eaten one too many jars of three-bean salad, try creating your own version for a change of pace. One option is to make it without the green or waxed beans and feature kidney beans and chickpeas instead. Of course, if you don't think that "three's a crowd," then go nuts and add a can of cut green beans to the mix.

One 15.5-ounce can chickpeas, drained (and rinsed, if possible)

One 15.5-ounce can kidney beans, drained (and rinsed, if possible)

One 2-ounce jar chopped pimientos, drained

1 tablespoon dehydrated minced onion

2 tablespoons white wine vinegar

1 teaspoon sugar

½ teaspoon salt

⅛ teaspoon cayenne pepper

¼ cup olive oil

1. In a large bowl combine the chickpeas, kidney beans, pimientos, and onion, then set aside.
2. To make the dressing, in a small bowl combine the vinegar, sugar, salt, and cayenne. Whisk in the oil to emulsify.
3. Pour the dressing over the salad and toss lightly to coat. Adjust seasonings to your tastes.

Makes 4 servings

"We're Not in Provence Anymore" *Salade Nicoise*

If you're inclined to eat canned tuna fish, this would be the salad to add it to since *salade nicoise* traditionally contains tuna. But try, just try, to enjoy it this way with chickpeas as the primary protein source. It's good for you. And surely everyone has an open jar of Dijon mustard—or some leftover deli packets of yellow mustard—just waiting to be used up in this salad!

1. In a large bowl combine beans, potatoes, tomatoes, chickpeas, and olives.
2. In a small bowl whisk together the remaining ingredients and add to the first mixture in the large bowl. Toss gently to combine. Adjust seasonings to your tastes.

Makes 4 servings

One 15-ounce can cut green beans, drained
One 16-ounce can diced white potatoes, drained
One 14.5-ounce can diced tomatoes, drained
One 15.5-ounce can chickpeas, drained (and rinsed, if possible)
One 4-ounce can pitted black olives, drained
¼ cup olive oil
1 ½ tablespoon white balsamic vinegar
1 teaspoon Dijon mustard
1 teaspoon dried basil
¼ teaspoon salt
Freshly ground black pepper

Crunchy Asian Salad with Peanut Dressing

A tangle of noodles with the peanut dressing upgrade. I've had dreams about this dish. And then made them come true.

½ cup peanut butter

3 tablespoons tamari or other soy sauce

2 tablespoons rice wine vinegar

½ teaspoon light brown sugar

¼ teaspoon red pepper flakes

⅛ teaspoon garlic powder

½ cup water

12 ounces rice noodles or linguine

1 tablespoon toasted sesame oil

One 8-ounce can sliced carrots, drained

One 8-ounce can water chestnuts, drained

One 8-ounce can straw mushrooms, drained

¼ cup dry-roasted peanuts

1. In a bowl combine the peanut butter, tamari, vinegar, sugar, red pepper flakes, and garlic powder, stirring to blend well. Add the water, stirring until smooth. Set aside.

2. Cook the noodles in a large pot of boiling water, according to package directions. Drain and rinse, if possible. Transfer to a large bowl. Toss with sesame oil to coat.

3. Add the carrots, water chestnuts, mushrooms, and peanuts to the bowl with the noodles. Add the reserved peanut sauce, tossing gently to combine.

Makes 4 servings

Hearts of Palm Salad with Limas, Black Olives, and Roasted Red Pepper Strips

We're talking colors, textures, and flavors with this knockout salad that is obscenely easy to put together. Just make sure you didn't skimp on the spices when you put together your secret disaster pantry stash.

1. In a large bowl combine the hearts of palm, lima beans, red peppers, and olives. Add the oil, lemon juice, chives, mustard, basil, oregano, salt, and pepper. Toss gently to combine.
2. Cover and set aside at room temperature for about 10 minutes to allow flavors to blend before serving.

Makes 4 servings

One 14-ounce can hearts of palm, cut into ¼-inch rounds
One 15-ounce can lima beans, drained (and rinsed, if possible)
One 8-ounce jar roasted red bell peppers, drained and cut into strips
¼ cup kalamata olives, pitted and sliced
3 tablespoons extra virgin olive oil
2 tablespoons fresh lemon juice
1 teaspoon dried minced chives
½ teaspoon dry mustard
½ teaspoon dried basil
⅛ teaspoon dried oregano
¼ teaspoon salt
⅛ teaspoon freshly ground black pepper

Sodium Watch

Put away your *fleur de sel* and *sel gris* for better days. Many canned and packaged foods are high in sodium, so you may not want to add yet more salt when you cook. That's when salt-free and low-sodium seasoning blends can help. Salt-free blends such as Mrs. Dash come in a wide variety of flavors from lemon pepper to spicy Cajun. Natural-food stores offer organic seasoning blends such as Herbamare, a blend of herbs and sea salt, which is lower in sodium than table salt. Note: When you do use salt, make sure it's iodized sea salt.

Condiments on Ice

If you stocked up on ice before the roof shingles hit the fan, you will have an advantage during the long lonely days ahead. Ice will allow you to keep some prepared foods longer, stretch the life of your condiments, and hold leftovers for another meal. Even without ice, condiments such as soy sauce, mustard, and ketchup will still be safe after a couple of days. But please, hold the mayo, and other condiments containing eggs or dairy products, and pitch them in the nearest trash bin.

Natural Preservatives

Foods containing animal products (meats, dairy, eggs) will be unsafe after just an hour or so at room temperature (see Appendix on page

231). Foods containing acids such as lemon juice and vinegar, like vinai-grette dressings, and pickled foods, such as capers and pickles, will last longer unrefrigerated if you keep them covered in the preserving liquid and with the lid on tight. Store them in the coolest spot possible.

Chapter 8

Full-Catastrophe Cooking: Soothing Soups

Soup is the ultimate comfort food, and when do you need comfort more than when a disaster turns your life upside down?

Many great soups normally must simmer for hours, but you don't have enough fuel for that. The solution is these simple soups, which use quick-cooking ingredients to produce rich-tasting results after only a few minutes of cooking time. Become the "Soup Nazi" of your neighborhood with these clever soups that can be made in minutes, but be careful not to make too much, as your refrigerator is out to lunch.

Soothing Soups

"Seeing Stars" White Beans and Greens Soup

Hot and Sour Soup

Black Bean Soup with a Whisper of Sherry

Shiitake Happens Mushroom Soup

Pretty Good Gumbo

Use-It-Up Minestrone Soup

Curry-Spiced Pumpkin Bisque with Coconut Milk

Comforting Corn Chowder

Artichoke, Shiitake, and White Bean Soup

Flaky Potato and Peanut Soup

Instant Vichyssoise

Emergency Gazpacho

To Make Vegetable Broth

Wondering how the fung-goo you're going to make vegetable broth, since everyone knows a good stock is the result of hours of simmering and reducing? Unless you have a working gas stove, you won't have the kind of fuel needed to simmer a pot of stock. So take stock of your Well-Tempered Pantry and choose from among the following items:

- canned broth
- broth in aseptic containers
- bouillon cubes
- powdered soup base

When a recipe calls for "2 cups vegetable broth," you can use any of the above items to make it. As with any packaged food, check the ingredients and buy the healthiest one. (Some are high in sodium and contain corn syrup, MSG, and other additives.) When using commercial broths, taste them for strength. Canned broth can be cut with water for a milder result. For example, if a recipe calls for four cups of broth, use one can (two cups) of broth plus two cups of water. This is also more economical, since some of these broths can be pricey. The most economical choice (which also economizes on space) is bouillon cubes or powdered soup bases. Our personal preference is Vogue Cuisine brand, especially their instant veggie base and instant vegetarian chicken base. Their products are made with mostly organic ingredients, have a good flavor, have no MSG or other hinky additives, and boast reduced sodium. One 12-ounce plastic jar is enough to make seventy-five cups of broth! Vogue products are available in natural-food stores.

"Seeing Stars" White Beans and Greens Soup

This homey soup makes a hearty and economical main dish. Stellini, small star-shaped pasta, add a touch of whimsy, but you can substitute another small soup pasta such as acine de pepe or pastene. Go continental under the stars. Light torches.

1 tablespoon olive oil
1 large garlic clove, minced
4 cups vegetable broth (see page 164)
One 16-ounce can cannellini beans, drained (and rinsed, if possible)
2 teaspoons dehydrated minced onion
¼ teaspoon red pepper flakes
¼ teaspoon dried oregano
Salt and freshly ground black pepper
¼ cup stellini or other small soup pasta
One 8-ounce can spinach, drained

1. Heat the oil in a large pot over medium heat. Add the garlic and cook until fragrant, about 30 seconds. Stir in the broth, beans, onion, red pepper flakes, oregano, and then salt and pepper to taste.
2. Bring to a boil, add the pasta, then reduce heat to low and simmer until the pasta is tender, about 6 minutes. Stir in the spinach. Serve hot.

Makes 4 servings

Hot and Sour Soup

This ingenious soup does spicy, pungent, and soothing all in one bowl. It's also a great way to get extra protein. Don't be afraid of tofu: It has no flavor of its own. Think of it as a highly charged ingredient that takes on the flavors of its surroundings.

1. If using dried mushrooms, soak them in a bowl of hot water for 30 minutes to soften. Drain and cut into julienne strips and set aside.

2. Heat the canola oil in a large saucepan over medium heat. Add the garlic and ginger, and cook until fragrant, about 30 seconds. Add the vegetable broth, onion, soy sauce, vinegar, sugar, chili paste, bamboo shoots, and the mushrooms. Bring to a boil over high heat, then reduce to a simmer and cook over medium heat until the mushrooms are tender, about 5 minutes. Add the cornstarch mixture, stirring to thicken slightly.

3. Add the tofu and the sesame oil and cook for 5 minutes until heated through.

Makes 4 servings

¼ ounce dried cloud ear mushrooms, or one 8-ounce can straw mushrooms, drained
1 tablespoon canola oil
1 garlic clove, minced
1 tablespoon grated ginger
4 cups vegetable broth (see page 164)
2 teaspoons dehydrated minced onion
3 tablespoons tamari or other soy sauce
2 tablespoons rice vinegar
½ teaspoon sugar
1 teaspoon Asian chili paste
One 8-ounce can bamboo shoots, drained and cut into julienne strips
2 teaspoons cornstarch dissolved in 1 tablespoon water
One 12-ounce aseptic package extra-firm tofu, cut into ¼-inch cubes
1 tablespoon toasted sesame oil

Black Bean Soup With a Whisper of Sherry

This satisfying stick-to-your-ribs soup is substantial enough to serve as a main course. Serve it with crackers or toasted bread for some crunch appeal. To make it creamier, puree up to half of the soup solids in a food mill and return it to the pot. A fresh onion and a carrot make good additions. If you have them, mince them finely and sauté them in the oil at the beginning of the recipe.

1 tablespoon olive oil
2 garlic cloves, minced
½ teaspoon dried oregano
½ teaspoon ground cumin
One 4-ounce can chopped
  mild green chiles, drained
Two 15.5-ounce cans black
  beans, drained (and rinsed,
  if possible)
One 14.5-ounce can diced
  tomatoes, drained
4 cups vegetable broth (see
  page 164) or water
¼ teaspoon celery salt
Freshly ground black pepper
2 tablespoons dry sherry

1. Heat the oil in a large pot over medium heat. Add garlic and cook 30 seconds or until fragrant. Stir in the oregano and cumin, then add the chiles, black beans, and tomatoes.
2. Add the broth and season with celery salt and pepper to taste. Simmer for 15 minutes to heat through and allow flavors to develop. Just before serving stir in the sherry.

Makes 4 servings

BLACK
BEANS

Shiitake Happens Mushroom Soup

Mushroom lovers will savor the rich flavor created by using a variety of mushrooms. Some people enjoy using dried mushrooms for their strong, earthy flavor. If you're not one of them, stick with the canned and jarred variety for a milder, yet still flavorful, soup. To make this soup a meal, add a can of white beans.

1. If using dried mushrooms, soak them in 2 cups hot water for 30 minutes. Thinly slice the mushrooms and set them aside. Discard the soaking water.

2. Heat the oil in a large pot over medium heat. Add the garlic and cook until fragrant, about 30 seconds. Stir in the sherry, onion, and thyme, and cook 1 minute longer.

3. If using dried mushrooms, add them to the pot along with the broth and bring to a boil. Reduce heat to low and add the rice, the straw mushrooms (if using), the shiitake and button mushrooms, parsley, then celery salt and pepper to taste. Simmer for 10 minutes. Adjust seasonings to your tastes.

Makes 4 servings

¼ ounce dried wild mushrooms, or one 8-ounce can straw mushrooms, drained

1 tablespoon olive oil

2 garlic cloves, minced

3 tablespoons dry sherry

1 tablespoon dehydrated minced onion

½ teaspoon dried thyme

4 cups vegetable broth (see page 164)

½ cup quick-cooking brown or white rice

One 10-ounce jar sliced shiitake mushrooms, drained

One 8-ounce jar sliced button mushrooms, drained

½ teaspoon dried parsley

¼ teaspoon celery salt

Freshly ground black pepper

Pretty Good Gumbo

The name of this spicy Cajun soup means "okra," although some people may choose not to include the mucilaginous vegetable when they make the soup. If you grew up in Louisiana, or have tasted authentic gumbo, this will put you in mind of better days. Say "mucilaginous" three times, real fast.

1 tablespoon olive oil

2 garlic cloves, minced

One 14.5-ounce can diced
   tomatoes, drained

One 6-ounce jar roasted red
   bell peppers, diced

1 tablespoon dehydrated minced onion

6 cups vegetable broth (see page 164)
   or water

One 15.5-ounce can kidney beans,
   drained (and rinsed, if possible)

½ cup quick-cooking rice

One 14-ounce can okra, drained and
   sliced (optional)

1 teaspoon dried thyme

1 teaspoon filé powder (optional)

¼ teaspoon celery salt

Salt and freshly ground black pepper

1 teaspoon Tabasco

1. Heat the oil in a large pot over medium heat. Add the garlic and cook for 30 seconds.

2. Stir in the tomatoes, bell peppers, onion, and broth and bring to a boil. Reduce heat to low and add the kidney beans, rice, okra (if using), thyme, filé powder (if using), celery salt, and then salt and pepper to taste.

3. Simmer, stirring occasionall, until rice is tender and soup is hot, about 5 minutes. Add the Tabasco and taste to adjust the seasonings.

Makes 4 servings

Use-It-Up Minestrone Soup

The classic Italian vegetable soup typically includes a wide variety of vegetables. Use up any fresh veggies or herbs still in decent shape by swapping them in for some of the canned vegetables in the recipe. Just slice the fresh veggies as thin as possible, so you can shorten cooking time. Cook any fresh vegetables in the broth first before adding the canned vegetables.

1. Heat the oil in a large saucepan over medium heat. Add the garlic and cook for 30 seconds.
2. Stir in the chickpeas, carrots, bell peppers, zucchini, green beans, tomatoes in their juices, broth, and onion. Season with parsley, basil, oregano, and then salt and pepper to taste. Bring to a boil, then reduce heat to low and simmer 15 minutes.

Makes 4 servings

1 tablespoon olive oil
1 large garlic clove, minced
One 15.5-ounce can chickpeas, drained (and rinsed, if possible)
One 8-ounce can sliced carrots, drained
One 6-ounce jar roasted red bell peppers, drained and diced
One 8-ounce can sliced zucchini, drained
One 8-ounce can cut green beans, drained
One 14.5 ounce can diced tomatoes, undrained
4 cups vegetable broth (see page 164)
1 tablespoon dehydrated minced onion
1 teaspoon dried parsley
1 teaspoon dried basil
¼ teaspoon dried oregano
Salt and freshly ground black pepper

Curry-Spiced Pumpkin Bisque with Coconut Milk

If you're in the mood for a savory, creamy soup, this is as close as you're going to get from a canned-goods pantry. If you like the flavor combination of curry and pumpkin, like we do, you'll make this treat even after the lights come on.

One 15-ounce can pumpkin puree
1 tablespoon curry powder
1 teaspoon light brown sugar
One 15-ounce can unsweetened coconut milk
1 cup vegetable broth (see page 164)
Salt and freshly ground black pepper
2 tablespoons pumpkin seeds (optional garnish)

1. Combine the pumpkin puree, curry powder, and sugar in a pot over medium heat. Whisk in the coconut milk a little at a time until mixture is smooth. Add up to a cup of the vegetable broth to achieve the desired consistency. Season with salt and pepper.
2. Simmer for 10 minutes to allow flavors to develop, stirring occasionally. Taste to adjust seasonings and serve hot, garnished with pumpkin seeds if desired.

Makes 4 servings

Comforting Corn Chowder

This sweet, satisfying chowder is made with a combination of canned whole kernel corn and creamed corn. The optional garnish of pimiento will add a dash of color and can give the impression around the neighborhood that you are a professional.

1. Combine both types of corn, potatoes, onion, celery salt, and broth in a large pot and bring to a boil. Reduce heat to medium and simmer, stirring frequently, for 5 minutes.
2. Add the milk and return to a simmer. Stir in the cornstarch mixture and mix until thickened slightly. Season to taste with pepper.
3. Ladle the soup into bowls and garnish with pimientos, if desired.

Makes 4 servings

One 15-ounce can corn, drained
One 15-ounce can creamed corn, undrained
One 16-ounce can diced white potatoes, drained
1 tablespoon dehydrated minced onion
¼ teaspoon celery salt
2 cups vegetable broth (see page 164)
1 cup milk or soy milk (see page 178)
1 tablespoon cornstarch combined with 2 tablespoons water
Freshly ground black pepper
One 2-ounce jar chopped pimientos, drained (optional)

Artichoke, Shiitake, and White Bean Soup

So delicious, it's hard to believe how quick and easy this soup is to make. And with elegant ingredients like artichokes and shiitake mushrooms, you may forget for a moment that dinner came from your emergency pantry. Jarred rather than dried shiitakes are used here for a more mellow flavor that allows the other ingredients to shine.

One 14-ounce can artichoke hearts, drained and chopped
One 15.5-ounce can Great Northern or other white beans, drained (and rinsed, if possible)
One 10-ounce jar sliced shiitake mushrooms, drained
1 tablespoon dehydrated minced onion
4 cups vegetable broth (see page 164)
1 teaspoon dried savory
1 bay leaf
Salt
Cayenne pepper

1. Combine all the ingredients in a large pot and bring to a boil. Reduce heat to low and simmer to heat through and develop the flavor, about 10 minutes.
2. Remove the bay leaf before serving. Serve hot.

Makes 4 servings

Flaky Potato and Peanut Soup

The secret ingredient in this rich, creamy peanut soup is the instant potato flakes. And it's not as flaky as you think, because of how well the flavors work together. The best part about this comforting soup is that the flavor can be altered to suit your mood. Feel like Thai? Add a smidge of lime juice, soy sauce, and chili paste. For an Indian flair stir in some curry powder. Or to simply jazz it up add a fresh or dried herb of choice.

1. Bring the broth to a boil in a large saucepan. Stir in the potato flakes until well blended. Reduce heat to low.
2. Place the peanut butter in a bowl and whisk in 1 cup of the hot broth mixture, blending until smooth. Stir the peanut butter mixture into the saucepan and add the celery salt, onion powder, and pepper to taste. Simmer 5 minutes to heat through and blend flavors.
3. Serve sprinkled with the chopped peanuts.

Makes 4 servings

4 cups vegetable broth
  (see page 164)
1 cup instant potato flakes
½ cup creamy peanut butter
¼ teaspoon celery salt
⅛ teaspoon onion powder
Freshly ground black pepper
¼ cup chopped dry-roasted
  peanuts

Instant Vichyssoise

Classic vichyssoise is served cold, but chilling this soup can be tricky without refrigeration, unless, of course, you're making this soup in the winter. During summer months you can chill it in the ice chest, if you have ice. Otherwise, room temperature will be the new chilled. To make a quick, hot potato soup instead, add a can of drained diced potatoes and heat it up in a saucepan.

2 cups vegetable broth (see page 164)
1 cup instant mashed potato flakes
2 cups milk or soy milk (see page 178)
Salt
Cayenne pepper
1 tablespoon dried chives

1. Bring the broth to a boil. Stir in the potato flakes, reduce heat to low, and simmer 5 minutes, stirring frequently. Remove from heat and set aside to cool.
2. Stir in the milk, and then season with salt and cayenne to taste. Sprinkle with chives and serve the soup as chilled as is practical.

Makes 4 servings

Emergency Gazpacho

Sometimes, even during an emergency, you just find yourself wishing for gazpacho. This quick and easy "salad soup" goes together in a flash. If you want to serve it as a main dish, just add a can of drained chickpeas or pinto beans.

1. Combine all of the ingredients in a large bowl and serve. Pass Tabasco at the table for those who like an extra jolt of heat.

Makes 4 servings

One 14.5-ounce can diced tomatoes, finely chopped
One 4-ounce jar roasted red bell peppers, chopped
One 4-ounce can chopped mild green chiles, drained
1 garlic clove, finely minced
1 tablespoon dehydrated minced onion
2 tablespoons chopped capers
1 tablespoon red wine vinegar
2 tablespoons olive oil
3 cups tomato or vegetable juice
½ teaspoon celery salt
1 teaspoon dried parsley
1 teaspoon Tabasco (optional)

Got Milk?

Soy milk in aseptic containers needs no refrigeration until it is opened, and can be a handy alternative to dairy milk. It is superior in flavor and texture compared to powdered dairy milk and has the added benefits of soy protein. Soy milk comes in these great little eight-ounce aseptic boxes—perfect to use in recipes. (You can also find rice milk packaged this way.) Soy milk is also available in a dry-powder form that can be reconstituted as needed with water. If you prefer, dairy milk is also available in aseptic containers and as a powdered nonfat dry milk. The recipes in this book can be made with either.

Survival Food Chic: Savvy Snacking

This chapter is about snacks. Not just any snacks but snacks that will propel you up through the Cheez-Its and potato chips of your old life to a new White Light of snack awareness. Would you believe Red Pepper Walnut Spread and Tapenade? Even better than that, this chapter offers gorp as an *amuse bouche* and tasty comfort foods that not only can satisfy your hunger but can actually help you relieve stress as you channel your energy into making an assortment of treats that are as much fun to make as they are to eat.

Savvy Snacking

Artichoke Dip
Red Pepper Walnut Spread
Texas Twister Caviar
Tapenade with Classy Crackers
Happy Trails Mix
Tropical Energy Balls
Peanutty Granola Balls
Almond Stuffed Dates
Gorp Redux

Artichoke Dip

This zesty dip is great served with crackers, chips, or bagel crisps.

1. Soak the sunflower seeds in hot water for 1 hour. Drain and set aside.
2. Use a hand chopper or grinder to finely mince the sunflower seeds and artichoke hearts. (If you don't have a grinder or chopper, use a sharp knife.) Transfer to a bowl.
3. Add a drop or two of Tabasco and salt to taste. Mix well to incorporate. Adjust seasonings to your tastes.

Makes 1 1/2 cups

¼ cup sunflower seeds
One 6-ounce jar marinated artichoke hearts, drained
Tabasco
Salt

Red Pepper Walnut Spread

The hearty flavor of this vibrant spread is as yummy on crackers as it is on toasted bread.

1 cup chopped walnut pieces
1 tablespoon olive oil
1 garlic clove, minced
One 6-ounce jar roasted red
bell peppers, drained
1 tablespoon dehydrated
minced onion
1 teaspoon dried parsley
Salt and freshly ground
black pepper

1. Finely grind the walnuts using a manual nut grinder or place in a plastic bag and crush them with a rolling pin or rubber mallet. Set aside.
2. Heat the oil in a small skillet over medium heat; add the garlic; cover; and cook until soft, about 1 minute. Transfer to a bowl.
3. Puree the roasted bell peppers through a food mill into the bowl with the garlic. Add the onion, parsley, reserved walnuts, and then salt and pepper to taste. Stir well to combine. Transfer to a small serving bowl.

Makes 4 servings

Happy Trails Mix

The combination of sweet and savory flavors and soft and crunchy textures makes this an ideal snack to perk you up in a variety of situations. Stash away an extra bag or two for when you need a healthy jolt. Seal it in airtight sandwich bags and keep in a reasonably cool spot. It will stay fresh for several days. This recipe can be easily halved.

1. Combine all the ingredients in a large bowl. Toss gently to combine.
2. Divide mixture into 10 small resealable plastic food-storage bags. Store in a cool, dry place.

Makes about 10 cups

2 cups mini pretzels
2 cups dry-roasted peanuts
1 ½ cups chocolate chips
1 ½ cups dried cranberries
1 ½ cups crispy cereal squares
1 ½ cups sunflower seeds or
pepitas (pumpkin seeds)

Tropical Energy Balls

When a tropical storm zaps your power, the experience can sap your personal energy as well, while you worry about when you can turn on your computer once again. Try these tasty treats to get you through the hot days and dark nights.

1 cup pitted dates or mixed dried fruit
1 cup walnut pieces
½ cup flaked coconut (plus more for rolling into balls)
1 tablespoon almond butter or other nut butter
½ teaspoon vanilla extract

1. Soak the dates or fruit in a bowl of water for 15 minutes.
2. While the fruit is soaking, use a hand chopper, knife, or rubber mallet to finely crush the nuts. Place the nuts in a bowl and add the coconut, almond butter, and vanilla. Incorporate with a pastry blender.
3. Coat a pair of scissor blades with nonstick cooking spray and snip the dates or fruit into the nut mixture with the scissors. Use the pastry blender or your hands to blend the mixture together.
4. Use your hands to shape the mixture into balls. Roll in additional coconut, if desired.

Makes about 16 pieces

Peanutty Granola Balls

Like a bite-size granola bar, these tasty morsels make terrific energy-boosting between-meal snacks. They also make a fun, hassle-free breakfast.

1. Use a pastry blender or whisk to combine the peanut butter, maple syrup, and juice until well blended.
2. Stir in the granola and mix until well blended.
3. Use your hands to roll into 1-inch balls and set on a plate. Roll in ground nuts, if desired.

Makes about 12 pieces

¼ cup peanut butter

2 tablespoons maple syrup

2 tablespoons apple juice (or other fruit juice)

1 ½ cups granola

½ cup ground peanuts or other nuts (optional)

Almond Stuffed Dates

Here's a recipe that's so easy, your dog could make it. Just two ingredients and takes about thirty seconds to make. Now, who said you're not a cook? When made with raw almonds, this snack is a favorite of raw foodists, because all the nutrients and enzymes stay intact, but you can also use dry-roasted or blanched almonds, if you prefer.

12 almonds
  (raw, dry-roasted, or blanched)
12 pitted dates

Stuff an almond into each of the dates. Arrange on a plate. Devour.

Makes 12 pieces

Gorp Redux

Any backpacker worth his hiking boots knows about gorp—"good old raisins and peanuts." Through the years creative riffs have incorporated nuts and dried fruit combos with chocolate chips and other yummy ingredients. This is our signature gorp, or, more accurately, "gobacch," for "good old blueberries, almonds, cranberries, chocolate, and hazelnuts." To show that you know how to be trendy, place two or three pieces of the mixture (a cranberry and two hazelnuts, for example) on salad plates and serve as an *amuse bouche* at the beginning of a meal.

1. Combine all the ingredients in a large bowl. Toss gently to combine.
2. Divide mixture into 5 small resealable plastic food-storage bags. Store in a cool, dry place.

Makes about 5 cups

1 cup white chocolate chips
1 cup sweetened dried cranberries
1 cup sweetened dried blueberries
1 cup slivered almonds
1 cup hazelnuts

Double-Duty Snack

Pistachios in the shell make a great snack food. They also give you something to do. This helps take your mind off your troubles and, since you need to open each nut one at a time, keeps you from scarfing down handfuls and spoiling your dinner.

For the Person Who Wants Everything

The truly cosmopolitan refugee can't resist the 11-in-1 Survival Lantern offered by the Sharper Image. The 8 ½-pound gadget features a 5 ¼-inch black-and-white TV screen, an AM/FM weather-band radio, fluorescent lamps, a spotlight, siren, and red blinking light. It also has a digital clock, thermometer, detachable compass, and sonic mosquito repeller. This little jewel operates on AC and DC adapters or 9D batteries. It costs about $80.

Chapter 10

Just Rewards: Dessert Every Day

I think of dessert as therapy on a plate (or in a bowl) because sweets are the ultimate comfort food when we need comfort the most. Even the experts agree that during emergency situations, a hoard of sweets is a good idea to help relieve the day-to-day stress. After all, "stressed" is "desserts" spelled backward. It can't be a coincidence.

This chapter provides easy recipes for great desserts made from your on-hand stash. Some of them are even healthy, though one doesn't often mention health in the same sentence as dessert, but all of them are homemade.

No doubt after reading this book you'll want to go out and stockpile Oreos, Ring Dings, and other store-bought obsessions, but let's face it, with those you get no say in how much hydrogenated fat, additives, or preservatives come with every bite. We advise: Stay in control by making it yourself.

Some of these recipes call for fruit, and you can use canned or dried. Hopefully you stocked up on both. If you still have fresh fruit on hand, save them to enjoy as a snack. You get more nutrients that way and can enjoy the true flavor and texture of the fruit uncomplicated by sugar and spice. If you tire of noshing on dried fruit, simmer them in sugar water for a lovely fruit macédoine that can be enjoyed for dessert or as a special topping for your breakfast oatmeal or pancakes.

Dessert Every Day

Strawberry Needles in White-Chocolate Toasted-Almond Haystacks

Darling Clementines with Pistachios and Cranberries

Skillet Peach Crumble

Fire-Roasted Blueberry Cobbler

No-Fuss Chocolate Fondue

Sweet Treat Chocolate Truffles

A Mere Trifle

Happy Granny's Ginger-Walnut Rum Balls

Pears and Peanuts with a Flourish of Chocolate

Strawberry Needles in White-Chocolate Toasted-Almond Haystacks

Finding a needle in a haystack was never so tasty. An unlikely quartet of ingredients? Sure, but wait until you taste them. Look for fruit leather near the canned and dried fruits in supermarkets and natural-food stores.

1 piece strawberry fruit leather
8 ounces white chocolate
½ cup toasted slivered almonds
1 ½ cups chow mein noodles

1. Use a pair of kitchen shears to cut the fruit leather into extremely fine strips, less than 1/16-inch thick. Set aside.

2. Melt the white chocolate in a metal bowl over a saucepan of boiling water.

3. When the chocolate is melted, stir in the almonds, noodles, and reserved fruit leather "needles." Mix well.

4. While still warm, use a teaspoon to drop the mixture into small mounds onto a baking sheet lined with parchment paper or waxed paper. (You can use your hands to create more haystacklike shapes, if you like). Set aside to firm up.

Makes about 24 pieces

Darling Clementines with Pistachios and Cranberries

Admittedly, canned fruit pales in comparison to fresh, but when it's all you've got, you must find ways to make the most of it. Pour on a splash of fragrant orange flower water (distilled from orange blossoms and available at gourmet markets), a sprinkle of pistachios, dried cranberries, and finish with a sprig of mint, and you've elevated this canned fruit to a gorgeous gourmet treat. Try this same treatment on canned apricots.

1. Arrange clementines in a bowl with 1/4 cup of their liquid. Sprinkle with pistachios and cranberries.
2. Splash with the orange flower water and lemon juice. Garnish with mint leaves, if desired.

Makes 4 servings

Two 8-ounce cans clementines, drained (reserve ¼ cup liquid)
¼ cup chopped pistachio nuts
2 tablespoons sweetened dried cranberries
2 teaspoons orange flower water (optional)
1 teaspoon lemon juice (optional)
Mint leaves, from your garden, if you have them (optional)

Skillet Peach Crumble

Similar to a fruit crisp, this dessert is made in a skillet on a stove top instead of in the oven. The basis of the crumble topping is healthful, toothsome oatmeal. Yum. For variety try it with apple pie filling.

⅔ cup rolled oats (old-fashioned) or quick-cooking oats

¼ cup light brown sugar or a natural sweetener

1 tablespoon peanut butter

1 tablespoon canola oil

1 teaspoon ground cinnamon

One 28-ounce can sliced peaches, drained

1. In a medium bowl combine the oats, sugar, peanut butter, oil, and cinnamon. Mix well and cook in a 10-inch skillet over medium heat until toasted, stirring frequently to avoid burning, about 5 minutes. Scrape topping mixture back into the bowl.

2. In the same skillet spread the peach slices in the same direction in concentric rows. Sprinkle the reserved topping on top of the fruit.

3. Cover and cook over low heat until hot, about 10 minutes.

Makes 4 servings

Fire-Roasted Blueberry Cobbler

It sounds improbable, but you can really make a darn good cobbler over an open flame. The heat bubbles up through the filling to cook the cakelike topping. Keeping a lid on things retains the heat. In a matter of minutes you have a fresh hot cobbler. During the last hurricane I recommended blueberry cobbler three meals a day every day, but the request was turned down.

1. Combine the pie filling, cinnamon, and lemon juice in a 10-inch skillet and place over a medium flame.
2. In a bowl combine the flour, sugar, baking powder, and salt. Stir in the milk and oil, mixing until just combined.
3. Spread the batter evenly over the blueberry mixture. Cover and cook until the batter becomes firm and cakelike, about 15 minutes. Turn off heat and let stand covered for another 5 to 10 minutes.

Makes 4 servings

One 16-ounce can blueberry
pie filling
1 pinch cinnamon
1 teaspoon lemon juice or
lemon zest
1 ¾ cup unbleached all-
purpose flour
½ cup sugar
2 teaspoons baking powder
1 pinch salt
1 cup milk or soy milk
2 tablespoons canola oil

No-Fuss Chocolate Fondue

Fondue is easy to assemble, fun to eat, and delicious in the bargain. What better way to while away the hours than by dipping chunks of cake, cookies, fruit, and pretzels in a pot of warm rich chocolate laced with your favorite liqueur?

8 ounces semisweet chocolate
½ cup milk or soy milk
3 tablespoons sugar
1 to 2 tablespoons liqueur of choice (optional; we like Frangelico)
Assorted canned and reconstituted dried fruit for dipping, cut into bite-size pieces as necessary (pears, pineapple, etc.)
Cake or cookies, cut into bite-size pieces
Pretzel sticks, etc.

1. Break the chocolate into pieces and place in a fondue pot. Light the Sterno, cover, and occasionally stir the chocolate until melted.
2. Blend in the milk and sugar. Stir in the liqueur. Cover and let the mixture continue to heat until the chocolate mixture is hot.
3. Arrange the "dippers" on plates and set them on the table with fondue forks or wooden skewers. Let everyone dig in. Try to avoid skewering each other.

Makes 4 to 6 servings

Sweet Treat Chocolate Truffles

In a perfect world you would refrigerate these little beauties for a while, just to help them firm up. But they are still amazingly delicious without chilling, and the ground nuts keep them from sticking to your fingers.

1. Melt the chocolate in a metal bowl over a saucepan with boiling water.
2. Remove from heat and stir in the sugar and peanut butter, mixing until well combined.
3. Use your hands to shape the mixture into 1-inch balls, and set on a plate lined with plastic wrap.
4. Roll the balls in the ground nuts and set aside in a cool spot, if possible, to firm up a bit.

Makes 10 to 12 pieces

½ cup semisweet chocolate morsels
½ cup confectioners' sugar
¼ cup peanut butter
⅓ cup ground dry-roasted peanuts

A Mere Trifle

The traditional English trifle is the jambalaya of the dessert world, made with a trifle of this and a trifle of that—usually cubed cake, pudding, and fruit— layered in a footed clear glass trifle bowl. You can make your own version of a trifle using whatever sweets you may have on hand. Make it in individual glasses if you prefer. If you have no pie filling, use jam; pureed, rehydrated dried fruits; or drained and chopped canned fruit.

**Three ½-inch slices pound
  cake or other cake, cubed
One 8-ounce jar strawberry
  fruit spread
3 oatmeal cookies, crumbled
Two ½-cup containers
  prepared vanilla pudding
1 chocolate bar**

1. In a clear glass bowl or in individual dessert glasses, layer the cake, fruit spread, cookies, and pudding.
2. Use a vegetable peeler to make chocolate shavings or curls, and sprinkle them on top of the trifle.

Makes 4 servings

Surviving Dessert

If you do not have a year's supply of Li'l Doofus Snack Cakes lining your walls, then a power outage gives you a great opportunity to eat healthier desserts. Remember fruit? As luck would have it some fruits actually hold up well at room temperature. Plan ahead to keep a good supply of apples, firm pears, green bananas (so they ripen slowly), and citrus fruit, among others. They can be delicious and fun to eat, either out of hand or cut up and served in a glass bowl.

Baking Without an Oven

At www.frybake.com you can find pots and pans for outdoor cooks that will work great over your emergency single-burner stove. However, any deep skillet will do, as long as it doesn't have plastic handles. They also carry a handy convection dome that can cut down your stove-top baking time by 30 percent. Also check out Coleman's propane- or gasoline-powered camp oven and camp coffeemaker. Visit www.coleman.com for details.

Chapter 11

Are We Having Fun Yet?

Another important challenge you'll face during your brave sojourn without electric power is the psychological albatross of boredom, discomfort, frustration, stress, and anxiety. Tempers can flare. Not just waiting in line for water, but around the house among people who are ordinarily nice to one another.

The stresses and strains can also plummet you into depression, into a black hole of mindless staring and bitterness that seems like it will never end. You had a modern, gadget-filled life once, and now you want it back. You want to attend concerts. Watch DVDs. Eat fresh food. You want the world to be normal again, and you want it now. You crave shopping or yearn to buy lumber and nails to start fixing up your house, but you can't drive anywhere. You resent that you had to cancel the Tuscany vacation that you had been planning for years. This is a chapter about how to tote all that emotional baggage.

Oh, the Stress!

After only two days without power, climate control seems like a dim memory. You live in a lightless silence. If it happens in summer, your skin is clammy, you stink, and you're "Evelyn Wood"ing the last chapters of a book before the sun goes down.

"Use the camping light."

"I can't *read* with the camping light, I've *told* you that."

"Try *anyway*."

"It gives me a *headache*."

"*Everything* gives you a headache."

"You wanna *eat* this book? It's Stephen King. You wanna *eat it*? *Huh?*"

In the event of a blackout that lasts longer than a day, you will experience a temporary loss of sanity. A hurricane, or some other whimsical notion of nature, can plague you for days. Four weeks after Hurricane Charley, there were still two hundred thousand people without power. Obviously, people whose houses counted among the fifty thousand that were destroyed, or nearly so, had more to worry about than keeping amused and making a great dinner, but millions of others found themselves playing a hot, grimy, intense game of nerves, which many people lost.

> ## A Fine Natural Stress Reducer
> Next time you feel stressed out, consider this natural remedy: a hot cup of organic chamomile tea and a tab of Xanax.

The frustration works its way from your skin and twitches there, just waiting until the next bureaucrat puts you on hold or the next pernicious youngster asks for the twentieth time when *SpongeBob* will come back on. You will wish for ways to maintain your equilibrium as you gaze repeatedly at the ruins of your neighborhood. And your only escape may be the back-yard, where you stare at what was once a flower garden for which you had just spent five hundred dollars on shrubs, annuals, perennials, and planters, now blasted to bits and dispersed by the winds. And, oh no, the birdhouse. Yes, the goddamn handmade birdhouse you bought from the master crafts-man in Oxford, Mississippi, as he spat tobacco; the one you debated with and negotiated (and won) the price thereof, and got it home all in one piece, but that your husband almost wrecked when he put it up, throwing his hammer, and taking the Lord's name in vain. And there it lies, the goddamn birdhouse, smashed flat by the grand cement lion lavabo that you had hung just so on the cottage wall. There have to be ways, you'll say. You will have to find a way not to kill each other. More important, after four days you will gladly pay one thousand dollars in cash just to take a hot shower.

During Hurricane Isabel we didn't have a lot of damage, but we had what we thought was a crisis. The tall pine tree that fell over our driveway was leaning on the heavy power lines, pulling them down like a country clothesline. This was at the corner of our house, and we feared the line might snap and start a fire—it's hard to sleep with the loblolly of Damocles poised over your house. The power company was useless. The automatic answering system gave you only two choices: If it's an emergency, press 1 and leave a message; for all other calls, press 2 and leave a message.

Please. Just one insurance story:

DAY ONE: Tried repeatedly to phone our insurance company (a nationally known company). Busy signal, all day.

DAY TWO: Put on hold for thirty minutes. Cut off. Called again. Put on hold for forty minutes. Finally talked to a living soul, who told us that they would arrange for a crane to get the tree off the power line. (The power company couldn't be bothered.)

DAY THREE: Still no crane. Called insurance company again. On hold. A different agent got on the line. We asked where the crane was, and he didn't know what we were talking about.

"No, *no,*" he scolded irritably. "We don't take care of that. You have to arrange for your own crane. Then we pay the bill." We then left messages on the answering machines of eight tree services.

DAY FOUR: Crane with an eighty-foot boom shows up—a miracle, considering the demand—lifts tree from power line as we watch breathlessly. (See Getting a Grip on p. 210.) Wrote check. We slept easier.

DAY FIVE: A deafening roar out front. A giant crane—large enough to lift the Triborough Bridge to the top of the Chrysler Building—pulls up to our house, barely squeezing under the power lines. Four service trucks arrive with it, and a pickup truck, all with Alabama plates. (For hurricanes, power crew$ come from all over to help.) These guys are tough. Built like professional wrestlers, their blond hair straggles to their shoulders. They are heavily tattooed and speak with moonshine accents. Two bumper stickers on one truck read, EVERYTHING I KNOW I LEARNED IN SUNDAY SCHOOL and YOU CAN'T HAVE TOO MUCH AMMO.

"*In*surance comp'ny sent us," one of them says, and Robin and I commence to explain what the insurance company told us. The men (one of whom had a raccoon tail woven into his mullet) had driven all the way from Chesapeake to reach us, and they wanted us to pay them, etc. It took an hour on the phone to straighten it out. The 'Bama boys were nice about it. Before they left on another insurance call fifteen miles away, I suggested that they call first.

Under these circumstances even the sweetest petunia among us can become a touchy, fire-breathing dragon, so it's important to find ways to relieve tension and keep occupied.

How to Relieve Stress

There are many ways to relieve stress. Sitting around with the power off is a perfect time to try some of these classics.

Deep Breathing: Tension creates rapid, shallow breaths. So, to relax, change the pattern of your breathing. Inhale slowly, hold your breath, and exhale slowly. Count to eight during each phase, and the temptation to strangle an errant official will pass.

Exercise and Stretching: Do calisthenics in your yard. If the streets are safe, walk around and compare damage reports. If a lot of people are worse off than you are, it can help you feel lucky and even magnanimous, if not damned well superior.

Massage: Every day take turns exchanging massages. Work the back of the neck and shoulders. Use thumbs and the heels of your hands. Massage anything you like.

Procreate: You can also lay the groundwork for an addition to your family. Or, if things are bad enough, begin the human race anew. (Statistics show an increase in births nine months after major blackouts.) Caution: Neighbors may decline to join you in this activity.

Yoga: There's no time like the present to practice this ancient form of exercise and mental discipline.

Take a Nap: Even a fifteen-minute nap can refresh you. For fun try your nap in unusual places: the floor, the backyard, the roof of the doghouse (Snoopy style), or on the dining-room table.

Visualize: Enjoy your memories of a time in the past when your toast popped out of your toaster, you were able to grumble about spam e-mail, and you could watch *Survivor!* on TV. Concentrate on the sights, smells, and sounds of the way life used to be. Or indulge your senses in something entirely new: the blessed absence of all the above.

Getting a Grip

It's well known that long-term stress exacerbates a number of medical and emotional problems. Stress plays a role in 50 to 80 percent of our illnesses today, and more than forty million of us take drugs to cope with it. Stressed-out people are anxious, exhausted, irritable, and feel awful most of the time. Stress also weakens the immune system, raises blood pressure, increases your susceptibility to illness, and can even impair your judgment in emergency situations. A bad mix for a natural disaster in anyone's book.

So, if you are stressed out to begin with, some random catastrophe throwing you into a world of discomfort and uncertainty is the last thing you need. Think of it—every aspect of your life will be on hold. If you are self-employed, you imagine your Giant Net Worth Gauge throbbing down like the mercury in a sphygmomanometer. But you can't afford to let "Life As I Knew It Before" dominate your thoughts. No. You have to let it go because now you have more important things to think about:

- **food, water, shelter**
- **safety for your household**
- **fighting off looters**
- **preventing injuries**
- **making fire**

Added to this can be a host of frightening, dangerous, or even tragic circumstances that are quite beyond the scope of this book. But even if your only problem is a lack of electric power, the days can drag on, frustrations can compound, and you can morph into a powder-keg banshee at the slightest provocation ("Hi, Dad," for example), and so forth.

With the power out for an extended period of time, you simply have to get a grip. Thousands of other people are in the same situation, so you can't expect the authorities to give you a lot of special attention or even be polite—they're stressed out too, because instead of dealing with their own homes, they are out there trying to deal with perhaps ten thousand that belong to other people. You may as well accept it up front that getting the power back on is going to take time, and you're going to have to do without things for a while. If you planned ahead—put together a pantry, gathered your Disaster Supply Kit, acquired an alternative method for cooking, and had your home secured—you're halfway there. Then, all you have to do is maintain a pinch of decorum as you endure:

- **unavailable or evasive authorities**
- **holding on the phone**
- **darkness and empty silence after the sun goes down**
- **loss of conveniences**
- **possible loss of water—no toilet, shower, or drinking water**
- **bored, irritable family members**
- **the burden of sitting still**
- **frustration**
- **cabin fever**
- **extreme temperatures (depending on your climate and the time of year)**

Cooking is one creative way to channel your futile rage and helpless frustration. Instead of sulking, whip up a batch of Moroccan-Spiced

Vegetable Stew or Fire-Roasted Blueberry Cobbler—it'll keep everyone busy and creative, especially if you've never cooked before.

You can't solve major problems through cooking, but you can glow with pride as you solve minor ones: sautéing garlic in a cast-iron skillet over a wood fire; using a shortcut for making a velouté sauce over a plumber's torch; frying up a righteous breakfast over the whisper of a blue flame; or serving a hot three-course dinner with only one burner. All this helps pass the time, mainly by keeping everyone working together. The more courses, the less time you have to gripe about your misery.

We are loath to admit that, on its own, cooking may not get you through the near annihilation of your house and neighborhood and the possible loss of your business, even though it has helped us through several natural disasters and miscellaneous extended blackouts. So, we'll share a secret: In addition to our Well-Tempered Pantry, we were glad to have some other diversions, to occupy us between meals.

Disaster Reading List, Part I
Books to Make You Feel Better

The Donner Party Chronicles by Frank Mullen
Gone with the Wind by Margaret Mitchell
The Perfect Storm: A True Story of Men Against the Sea by Sebastian Junger
Genesis 6:9 by You-Know-Who (also see the same Author's *Book of Job*)
A River Runs Through It and Other Stories by Norman Maclean
The Revelation of John by John
The Wizard of Oz (esp. in the Midwest) by L. Frank Baum
The Worst-Case Scenario Survival Handbook by Joshua Piven and David Borgenicht

Reading

When the last hurricane hit, I'd been so busy rewriting my novel, I realized that it had been months since I'd read one. On a trip to Manteo, North Carolina (home of Andy Griffith), that summer, I had picked up Toni Morrison's *Sula,* her second book from 1973 that I'd been meaning to read since 1973. Thank you, Professor Morrison, for my daylong eavesdrop on Sula's world! Robin and I caught up on a lot of reading after those storms. Reread *Intruder in the Dust*, wept over *Romeo and Juliet*, and even dug out an old dog-eared Gary Larson cartoon collection. (Remember the one where this goofy guy is walking beneath a piano, and God is at his computer about to push the Smite button? It helped us guffaw at our plight.)

Disaster Reading List, Part II
Books to Keep You Busy

Brain Teasers by Kiran Srinivas
Field Guide to the Apocalypse by Meghann Marco
How to Make Love All Night (And Drive a Woman Wild) by Barbara Keesling
Knitting with Dog Hair by Kendall Crolius and Anne Black Montgomery
The New York Times Ultimate Crossword Omnibus by Will Shortz, editor
Very Naughty Origami by Nick Robinson

Children Underfoot

For self-defense you really ought to keep a variety of games handy. Whatever you're going through you can bet that the children are worse off than you are. After all they haven't yet matured enough to worry themselves into a quivering mass over a Visa bill. But that's not all. Unless you filled your Well-Tempered Pantry with junk food, they have suddenly been cut off from their 100 percent sugar diet. There are no Xbox or PS2 games, no videos, cable TV, computers, or Internet. They can't even use their cell phones, because the towers don't work. The streets are covered in branches and junk, so no skateboarding. Live power lines are dangling everywhere, so, even if you're tempted, you can't send them out to ride their bikes. You also can't let them wander around on foot, lest you find yourself posting bond because they were picked up for looting or trespassing.

Yes, it's best to keep lots of games around for the kiddies. If they're old enough, you can even press them into helping with the cooking. Give them jobs. Let them know they're important to the family's survival. Who knows, they might take it seriously. Teach the little princess in your life how to muck out the family Porta Potti. Show your young running back how to sauté shallots. Be positive. Change is in the wind.

Disaster Reading List, Part III
Books for Teenagers

Abstinence: The New Sexual Revolution by Marilyn Morris
The Complete Stories by Franz Kafka
How to Read a Book by Charles Van Doren and Mortimer J. Adler
Math for Fun Projects (Math for Fun) by Andrew King and Tony Kenyon
Statistical Abstract of the United States: The National Data Book by the
    Bureau of the Census

Gaming

The adults also have to keep busy. With a deck of cards, you can play pinochle, poker, canasta, or gin rummy. But with several decks of cards, you can each play solitaire anytime you're not speaking to one another. Have Monopoly and Scrabble at the ready along with other games of skill and chance. Games that take time to play can eat up the hours. Idea: Play blackjack to see who will rake the yard, who will saw up branches, or who will drag the neighbor's lawn mower out of your swimming pool.

Misery Loves Company

Without regard to species, disasters bring out cooperation and charity among neighbors. Back in 1989, as Hugo's winds blasted the houses on Sullivan's Island, South Carolina, the Baker family was huddled in the corner of their living room, fearful that they had made the wrong decision by staying home. Dad, Mom, and the two children were riding out the storm by the stone fireplace, when they heard a scratching at the front door. The screech was too regular to be a tree limb, so, cautiously, Dad opened the door and peeked out. Bracing the door against the wind, they watched gape-jawed as a family of squirrels (the Citelluses) ambled in. A dad, a mom, and two baby squirrels had applied for asylum and a door had opened unto them. The

Citellus family stepped cautiously along the wall and huddled in the corner across the room from the humans. While the tempest raged outside, neither species bothered the other, but shared the shelter and some mutual respect until the worst had passed. Once the door opened again, the refugees scampered to their tree, and life returned to normal.

During Isabel we got to know our neighbors for the first time in eleven years. That's right. My wife and I tend to scurry into and out of our house like muskrats, never looking to the right or left, anxious to get back to our work. In a rare face-to-face encounter with a neighbor, the breath stops and smiles strain. There's a chuckled, "Hi," "Hi there," or "Nice weather." But after the hurricane everything changed. Half our neighborhood had ignored the warning to evacuate, and, like survivors emerging from the ruins after the B-52s have passed over, we picked our way into our front yards, blinking around in slow motion at the wreckage, smiling the grateful smile of gamblers who have beaten the odds.

We had no idea that across the street was a retired engineer. Next door, a pilot for the Navy SEALs. Next to him was a medical doctor, and beyond were a police officer and a retired high-steel worker.

"And what do *you* do, Mr. and Mrs. Robertson?"

"Well, we write down words. Sort of on paper."

"I mean for your *job*. Your *work*."

"Well, sometimes people pay us for it."

Four houses down I actually discovered a distant relative—the guy's great-great-grandparents were also my great-great-grandparents, who had lived in the state of Maine around 1888. Small world.

In the face of adversity people's hearts open wide. One guy brought his chain saw around to cut up problem limbs and branches. Another acquired a generator big enough for four families to run their refrigerators and watch a little TV. Everybody contributed with their lawn-mower gas to fuel the generator, and it worked great until the do-it-yourself tank farm ran dry. Gas stations can't pump gas without electricity.

Another story comes to mind from Hurricane Hugo about a reclusive cook forced by circumstances to feed the multitude. He was not a man of words and still suffered from some unexplained terror he'd endured in Vietnam. Soft-spoken and pathologically shy, except when barking orders behind the cooking line, he found everyone in his devastated neighborhood unable to cope or organize themselves. They were all looking to him.

Painfully he came out of his shell and took over. Ordered everyone to bring out their charcoal grills and line them up. He had them empty their refrigerators and bring out their salad fixings, condiments, bowls, plates, wines, and serving sets. He created a cooking line. From passersby he drafted a team: a sommelier, a garde-manger, a sous-chef, grill cooks, and waiters. Tables were set up inline for an impromptu al fresco banquet. People came from blocks away and ate royally while the food lasted, and something inside him that had been terribly broken for twenty years began to heal.

Another way to get your mind off your own misery, therefore, is to spread that misery around. Meet people. See who needs what. Let others know what you need. Let the Disruptive Event turn your artificial community into a real one. Make friends as you share resources and lend a hand. You can also organize group games. Hold your own church service, prayer meeting, powwow, coffee klatch, sewing circle, sweat lodge, or encounter group. Or just pool your groceries, prepare a feast, break out the wine, and throw the best block party any of you will ever see again.

Psychological Tools

Last summer some new acquaintances, Clifford and Brooke, invited us over for dinner with encouragement to come hungry. Upon our arrival we couldn't help but notice the place settings on the dinner table. Colorful Majolica positioned on silver chargers. Salad plates. Bread-and-butter plates. Long-stemmed goblets for water, and other glasses for wine and champagne. A regiment of silverware heralded the bounty of courses to come. In the center of the plates stood starched napkins in the form of perfectly folded cardinal's hats.

Robin and I exchanged glances. It seemed we were in for the equivalent of a state dinner. It would be a feast to challenge Jacques Pépin, humble

Wolfgang Puck, silence Emeril Lagasse, and dispatch Anthony Bourdain to the medicine cabinet.

We began with dishes of cocktail olives—and saltines. Cool. Retro. Minimalist. We hadn't eaten since breakfast, but we didn't want to fill up. Next came a salad that Brooke tossed tableside and rationed out onto salad plates. The spartan servings, we reasoned—after thirty-three years, Robin and I now reason together—were merely a precursor to more sumptuous courses that would follow.

"More salad?"

"No. Thanks." We grinned, saving room for dinner.

Next came soup. Tomato soup. Tomato soup with some uncooked green pepper bits bobbing for air at the surface. Robin and I each washed a spoonful over our tongues, eyeing each other with the same dreadful thought.

"The soup tastes like dishwater."

We felt relieved that we could down it.

"Surely you'll have more *soup,*" sang Brooke afterward, but we didn't want any more of the toxic fluid, especially with dinner waiting in the wings.

"No. No."

Brooke departed for the kitchen, and we chatted with Clifford as he opened more wine. But Brooke returned in a flash with a rattling coffee tray.

"For dessert we have fruit and coffee," she announced. "Dig in."

Robin and I had the same thought: "But where's dinner?"

We each took a little dish of the fruit—six grapes, two slices of kiwi fruit, and some fresh strawberries—and sorted through the silverware to find the proper spoon. The fruit was gone in a few gulps. We drained our coffee cups. Admired the nearby impatiens. Smiled at our hosts and each other. Then we realized that there would be no more courses. When we got home, we made a hearty meal and howled tearfully about the cardinal's hat napkins. Next morning we spent hours trying to master the fold and realized that the activity can provide a splendid psychological tool for battling tedium during a power outage.

Artfully folded napkins are a dead giveaway that you are a cultured person with nothing to do. But even if you aren't, there's no denying that a well-set table without folded napkins is like a chain saw without two-stroke oil.

When there's no electricity, and your life seems light-years from being refined, perhaps that's the best time to consult the following directions and fold yourself some festive napkins. It's just one more way to thumb your nose at fate. You may be eating lukewarm beans, but darn it, your table is set with the best damned napkins this side of the Seine. It's also fun and educational for the kids—something you can learn together as a family. Best of all, after the lights come back on, it's a treasured skill that you will use for years to come.

"Yes," you can say proudly, as guests drool over your perfectly executed tri-folds, "I taught myself that particular napkin fold during Hurricane Yvonne back in '05."

For your first foray into the art of napkin folding, I've chosen three moderately challenging folds. Let's start with the pyramid. A starched cloth napkin is, of course, best. But if all you have are paper napkins, you can certainly practice with those. Naturally, the sturdier the napkin, the better your folds will turn out.

The Pyramid

1. With the napkin lying flat like a diamond before you, fold the top point down to meet the bottom point.
2. Fold the upper right and left points down to meet the bottom point.
3. Carefully turn the napkin over and fold the bottom point up to the top point.
4. Fold the lower left corner to meet the right corner. Stand the napkin in the center of a dinner place, like a tent, pointing toward the guest.

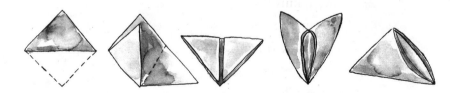

The Rose

The rose fold is perfect for an event in which each guest receives a token gift—the gift is placed in the center of the napkin after it is folded.

1. Lay napkin out flat and fold all four corners to the center.
2. Repeat step one.
3. With care, turn folded napkin over. Fold all four corners yet again to the center.
4. Holding the center down with your finger, reach beneath each corner and pull out a "petal." Shape the flower with your fingers and place a token gift in the center. (You can choose an AA battery, a book of matches, or, for nostalgia, a small lightbulb.)

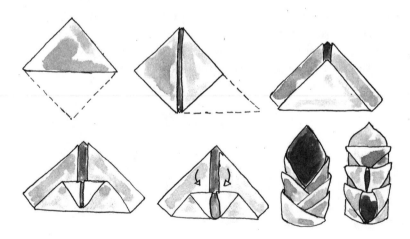

The Cardinal's Hat

You'll need a large napkin for this standing napkin fold.

1. With the napkin lying flat like a diamond before you, fold the bottom point up to meet the top point.
2. Fold the left and right corners up to meet the top point.
3. Make a cuff by turning the bottom up once about one or two inches, depending on the size of the napkin. Fold up again another inch or two.
4. Carefully turn the napkin over and fold the left and right sides toward the center, tucking the left corner into the right side of the cuff.
5. Stand the napkin on its cuff and pull the two top corners out and down.

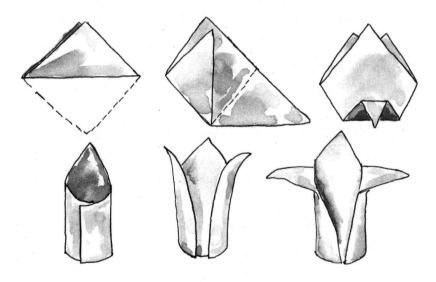

Overdoing Your Table

Now that you've mastered some impressive napkin folds, you're probably itching to set a table beautiful enough to feature them. So, let's get right to it.

Study the following diagram for a formal table setting. You can trust this diagram because it was provided by the International Guild of Professional Butlers (www.butlersguild.com/guests/table_settings/formal_dinner.html). While trying not to dwell on the hot dogs and beans you may be serving, carefully observe the placement of dishes, glasses, and utensils. It's *very* important that this be done right.

Whether you are just plain obsessive-compulsive or would like to steer your life in a new direction, follow these guidelines as you set up your backyard picnic table or sheet of plywood. The Butler's Guild is perfectly clear regarding the way in which the places are set: "Every place setting should be exactly the same, to the millimeter. An inexperienced butler might use some measuring device."

So, let's say some neighbor calls you out because he noticed through binoculars from his second-story bedroom window that you used an engineer's scale to properly place the aperitif flutes. Don't worry. He's obviously the one who is insane, and you should call the police at once. While waiting for the authorities to take care of that "little problem" next door, don't suffer needlessly over the fact that your paper plates, napkins, and cutlery are left over from your child's third birthday party. You are in an emergency situation and desperately

A. Napkin

B. Service plate

C. Soup bowl

D. Bread-and-butter plate
   with butter knife

E. Water glass

F. Wine glass

G. Wine glass

H. Salad fork

I. Dinner fork

J. Dessert fork

K. Knife

L. Teaspoon

M. Soup spoon

trying to save your sanity here. Have fun. Impress your neighbors (anyone left who hasn't been detained by the police). After this is all over, whenever they see you, they will probably look away uncomfortably, but take it from us, those captious curmudgeons are merely jealous.

Where to Place the Cutlery?

Readers who were quick to judge the author as negligent for omitting instructions for proper table service in the main text of this guide will wax penitent upon seeing them here. According to the International Guild of Professional Butlers, you wouldn't want to be caught neglecting even one of these rules when setting cutlery on a table:

- The handles will be one inch from the edge of the table.
- The two outermost pieces are used first.
- A soup spoon may go between knives if there is an appetizer before the soup.
- The butter knife on the bread plate has the blade face toward the center of the plate.
- Only the soup course has one piece of flatware; all others have two. A salad should be torn into bite-size pieces, but a knife may be used to push the food onto the fork.

A trifle, you say? Not in the least. And, besides, it eats up time.

During Hurricane Isabel we compromised by using disposable dinner-ware for breakfast, lunch, and snacks. Really. And it felt *good*. We did, however, reserve the "good dishes" for dinner. In our case, we were blessed with running water, so to keep from going nuts, we were able to incorporate hand-washing dishes as part of our "busywork" each day. Actually, after a day we had to wash dishes with the garden hose out in the yard because the electric garbage disposal clogged from washing dishes in the sink. So we set up a trio of dishpans in the backyard, one filled with the dirty dishes, one for rinsing, and one for draining.

On the sixth day without electricity we sat reading at the patio table, sweating beneath the umbrella, staring into the humid air. We were about to make lunch when we noticed a change in the air. It wasn't a new something; it was the *absence* of something. The noise had cranked down by sixty decibel. Someone had turned off a generator. Then another. Then there was silence. Our neighbor poked his grinning face above the fence.

"The power's back on."

"Really?"

"No kidding. We're watching *SpongeBob*!"

Like Gollum in pursuit of the Ring, we raced back inside and turned on every light in the house. Flipped on the computer to check e-mail. Turned on the TV. Listened to the stereo. Browsed the Web. We reveled in the return of our precious work and play. Our beloved gadgets. Back again was our electric stove. Back again were the reality shows, the commercials, the spyware, the pop-ups, the talking heads, VH1, Top 40, golden oldies, and movies. We hurried to catch up on business e-mail, to get back to our manuscripts and correspondences. Back to the rat race and responsibility and the nine-to-five pressure of daily life. Everything came back when the power lines hummed once again, and only then did we realize how much we had grown while the electricity was off.

But Isabel had given us another benefit. Hiding under her malevolent skirt was the idea for this book—a humble volume written by two people who figured out a way to maximize comfort and eat impossibly good meals after cruel natural circumstances had rendered them powerless. We herewith pass this wisdom on to you.

APPENDIX

Food Safety During an Emergency

For more information, visit the U.S. Department of Agriculture Food Safety and Inspection Service Web site at www.fsis.usda.gov/Fact_Sheets/keeping_food_safe_during_an_emergency/index.asp.

Did you know that the loss of power could jeopardize the safety of your food? Knowing how to determine if food is safe and how to keep it safe will help minimize the potential loss of food and reduce the risk of food-borne illness. This fact sheet will help you make the right decisions for keeping your family safe during an emergency.

ABCDs of Keeping Food Safe in an Emergency

Always keep meat, poultry, fish, and eggs refrigerated at or below 40 degrees Fahrenheit, and frozen food at or below 0 degrees Fahrenheit. This may be difficult when the power is out.

Keep the refrigerator and freezer doors closed as much as possible to maintain the temperature. The refrigerator will keep food cold for about four hours if it is unopened. A full freezer will hold the temperature for approximately forty-eight hours (twenty-four hours if it is half-full) if the door remains closed. Obtain dry or block ice to keep your refrigerator as cold as possible if the power is going to be out for a prolonged period of time. Fifty pounds of dry ice should hold a full eighteen-cubic-foot freezer for two days. Plan ahead and know where dry ice and block ice can be purchased.

Be prepared for an emergency by having items on hand that don't require refrigeration and can be eaten cold or heated on the outdoor grill. Shelf-stable food, boxed or canned milk, water, and canned goods should be part of a planned emergency food supply. Make sure you have ready-to-use baby formula for infants, and pet food. Remember to use these items and replace them from time to time. Be sure to keep a handheld can opener for an emergency.

Consider what you can do ahead of time to store your food safely in an emergency. If you live in a location that could be affected by a flood, plan to store your food on shelves that will be safely out of the way of contaminated water. Coolers are a great help for keeping food cold if the power will be out for more than four hours—have a couple on hand along with frozen gel packs. When your freezer is not full, keep items close together—this helps the food stay cold longer.

Digital, dial, or instant-read food thermometers and appliance thermometers will help you know if the food is at safe temperatures. Keep appliance thermometers in the refrigerator and freezer at all times. An appliance thermometer will always indicate the temperature in the refrigerator and freezer no matter how long the power has been out. The refrigerator temperature should be 40 degrees Fahrenheit or below; the freezer, 0 degrees Fahrenheit or lower. If you're not sure a particular food is cold enough, take its temperature with a food thermometer.

RESOURCES DIRECTORY

I. FOOD AND COOKING SUPPLIES

Nonperishable Foods

The Mail Order Catalog for Healthy Eating

A large variety of canned heat-and-serve vegetarian meats, boxed mixes for veggie burgers, ribs, and wheatmeat. Dehydrated textured soy protein in granules, chunks, strips, vegetarian jerky, and veggie pâtés. Also, specialty items such as fair-trade organic chocolate bars and vegan marshmallow crème.

Phone: 800-695-2241

www.healthy-eating.com

BulkFoods.com

Loads of dried nuts, fruits, and vegetables, including mixed vegetables, broccoli, asparagus, and carrots. Tomato powder, dried mushrooms (from sliced white to black trumpet), TVP (textured vegetable protein), soup bases, snack mixes, and more.

Phone: 419-324-0032

E-mail: vip@bulkfoods.com

www.bulkfoods.com

Retort-Packaged Meals

TheEpicenter.com

Distributes a variety of MREs and freeze-dried meal products

> Phone: 541-684-0717
> E-mail: bjnelson@TheEpicenter.com
> www.TheEpicenter.com

HeaterMeals

> Phone: 800-503-4483 (USA only) or 513-772-3066
> E-mail: info@heatermeals.com
> www.heatermeals.com

Homeland Preparedness

> Emergency supplies, disaster kits, and survival gear
> Phone: 800-350-1489
> E-mail: customerservice@homelandpreparedness.com
> www.homelandpreparedness.com

Major Surplus and Survival

> A good source for military-style MREs
> Phone: 800-441-8855 or 310-324-8855

E-mail: info@majorsurplusnsurvival.com

www.majorsurplusnsurvival.com

Mountain House

Freeze-dried foods for more than thirty years

    Phone: 800-547-0244

    E-mail: MH-info@ofd.com

    www.mountainhouse.com

Nitro-Pak Preparedness Center, Inc.

Offers a variety of freeze-dried food products, including seventy-two-hour survival kits aimed toward executives. Kits are available for one, two, and four individuals

    Phone: 800-866-4876

    www.nitro-pak.com

Saratoga Trading Company

Survival kits, food, water, and communications products for hurricanes and other disasters

    Phone: 800-773-5331

    E-mail: sales@saratogatradingcompany.com

    www.saratogatradingcompany.com

Portable Stoves

Most of the camp stoves described in Chapter 2 can be found through your local camping, sporting-goods, or outfitter store. You can also acquire the recommended single-burner butane stove from any of these sources:

www.preparedness.com

www.cooking.com

www.chefscatalog.com

Glomate

Glomate (Model GM-1600). A 7,517 BTU butane stove with rigid carrying case. Has autoignition with autosafety shut-off. Costs about $65. Uses eight-ounce disposable butane canister, sold on Web site.

E-mail: glomate@bellatlantic.net

www.glomate.com

Cadac Grills

Cadac Safari Chef Portable Gas Grill (Model 6526). This versatile grill uses propane and folds up into a carrying bag. It offers five different cooking surfaces, including roasting, grilling, and frying. It even provides a wok. Check local hardware stores and home centers or online. Costs about $70 to $90.

www.backyardcity.com

Century Tool & Manufacturing Company, Inc.

Century 2-Burner Propane Camping Stove (Model 4560). Two 10,000 BTU burners provide a large, stable cooking surface. It uses a 16.4–ounce propane cylinder but can easily be converted to bulk cylinder operation. The company also offers a variety of single-burner propane stoves for less than $30.

Phone: 800–435–4525

E-mail: wkeating@centurytool.biz

www.centurycamping.com

The Coleman Company, Inc.

Coleman Two-Burner Propane Stove (Model 5423E700). This familiar green metal camp stove has been around since the 1920s and provides 21,000 BTU when only the main burner is in use. The unit boils one quart of water in five minutes and costs about $60. They also make a butane-fired kettle for instant hot water and a folding camp oven.

Phone: 800–835–3278

E-mail: consumerservice@coleman.com

www.coleman.com

Mountain Safety Research (MSR)

Mountain Safety Research (MSR) DragonFly Stove (Model 311030). This stove weighs only 17.1 ounces and folds down to one-third of its working size. It brings water to a boil in three and a half minutes and costs about $110. The fuel canisters also fit other threaded butane stoves. One canister of MSR IsoPro fuel should be sufficient to boil water for two people over four days in summer.

Phone: 206-505-9500 or 800-531-9531

E-mail: info@msrgear.com

www.msrgear.com

Food Dehydration

Books on dehydrating: *Mary Bell's Complete Dehydrator Cookbook* by Mary Bell and Evie Righter (Morrow, 1994); *Backpack Gourmet* by Linda Frederick Yaffe (Stackpole Books, 2002). In addition, many raw or living-food cookbooks have fairly comprehensive sections on dehydrating food.

Web site on dehydrating: www.food-dehydrator-store.com. Reviews of the best dehydrators, comparison chart, guide, and articles.

Food dehydrators: Prices on dehydrators begin at around $40, but don't expect them to perform as well as the $200 Excalibur brand. Check out comparison Web sites, like bizrate.com, for dehydrators in a wide price range.

H. SURVIVAL SUPPLIES

The following companies provide emergency kits for home, office, and car, including prepacked foods, first aid, and safety equipment. The individual descriptions highlight additional specific features offered by that company.

The American Red Cross

Offering inexpensive first-aid and preparedness items online. Kits include battery-powered flashlights, radios, blankets, food bars, gloves, etc. You can purchase online or contact your local Red Cross office.

www.redcross.org (click store)

DisasterNecessities.com

Emergency equipment and food storage. Seventy-two-hour kits, water storage supplies, first-aid kits, and educational materials.

Phone: 801–361–7017

E-mail: help@DisasterNecessities.com

www.disasternecessities.com

Emergency Preparedness Center

Emergency survival kits for home, car, school, office. Kits for individuals and two to four persons.

Phone: 435-654-3447

E-mail: contact-us@areyouprepared.com

www.areyouprepared.com

Homeland Preparedness (See Retort-Packaged Meals above.)

Nitro-Pak Preparedness Center, Inc. (See Retort-Packaged Meals above.)

Ocean Air Associates

Survival kits along with alternatives for heat and light, clean-air canisters, emergency foods (including kosher), and baby-related items. Kits for outdoors also available.

Phone: 732-987-7047

E-mail: info@B-Prepared.com

www.b-prepared.com

Quake Kare, Inc.

Provides emergency survival kits, including fanny packs, food, and solar and hand-crank lights and radios. Kits are available for earthquakes, hurricanes, fires, floods, and other disasters.

Phone: 800-277-3727

E-mail: Info@QuakeKare.com

www.quakekare.com

SafetyMax

Offers a full line of first-aid, survival, and safety products and training services. Survival equipment for the office, kits for first responders and backpackers, and survival kits for two to ten people.

Phone: 800-585-8506

E-mail: info@safetymax.com.

www.safetymax.com

Saratoga Trading Company

(See Retort-Packaged-Meals above.)

III. IMPORTANT AGENCIES

For information about hurricanes

NOAA/National Weather Service

National Centers for Environmental Prediction

National Hurricane Center/Tropical Prediction Center

www.nhc.noaa.gov

For information about tornadoes

NOAA/National Weather Service

National Centers for Environmental Prediction

Storm Prediction Center

E-mail: spc.feedback@noaa.gov

www.spc.noaa.gov

For tornado information by state

www.disastercenter.com/tornado.html

For information about earthquake activity

U.S. Department of the Interior

Earthquake Hazards Program

http://earthquake.usgs.gov

For information on investigations into power blackouts

Federal Energy Regulatory Commission

Phone: 202-502-8680 or 866-208-3372 (toll free)

E-mail: customer@ferc.gov

www.ferc.gov/cust-protect/moi/blackout.asp

American Red Cross National Headquarters

Phone: 202-303-4498 or 866-GET-INFO/866-438-4636 (disaster assistance info) or 800-HELP-NOW/800-435-7669 (donations)

Federal Emergency Management Agency (FEMA)

Phone: 202-566-1600 or 800-480-2520 (to order publications)

E-mail: FEMAOPA@dhs.gov

www.fema.gov

Your Emergency Numbers Directory

Record important phone numbers here,
so they will be handy in case of an emergency.

Ambulance	911	Federal Emergency Management	
Fire	911	Agency (FEMA)	(202) 566-1600
Police	911	American Red Cross	
Family Physician _____		(local chapter) _____	
Local Hospital _____		Personal Trainer _____	
Power Company _____		Psychotherapist _____	
Gas Company _____		Life Coach _____	
Water Company _____		Massage Therapist _____	
Home Insurance _____		Ear Candler _____	
Auto Insurance _____		Cuppist _____	
		Past-Life Regressionist _____	

Notes